Praise for *Oscar López Rivera*

The story of Puerto Rican
in this book is a story of the lengths to which our government will go to punish and silence voices of liberation. But it is also the story of the courage of one man who perseveres in his hunger and thirst for justice. His witness—over thirty-one years in the worst prison circumstances the federal government could inflict on him—will inspire everyone who comes to know him.

—Bishop Thomas Gumbleton, founding president, Pax Christi USA

Between Torture and Resistance is a narrative about years of courage, love for one's people, suffering—offering that most precious thing we can count on during our path through the world: the offering of life. Listening to Oscar's voice in this book makes something clear that one such as Nelson Mandela would know well: his sense of liberty has not been extinguished by the jailers' bars or the torturers on call. Our dear Luis Nieves Falcón, exemplary servant and tireless worker for the freedom of our homeland, has—in this book—continued Oscar's struggle against imperialism. We cannot underestimate the powers of the narrative, of the word, that above all provides strength for new generations. *Between Torture and Resistance* is such a book and should be read by all people who cherish freedom and dignity.

—Celina Romany-Siaca, former president, Puerto Rican Bar Association

With over thirty-one years behind bars for the political thought-crime of "seditious conspiracy," Puerto Rico's Oscar López Rivera spotlights an urgent challenge to U.S. jurisprudence; he is supported by politicians and civic leaders from every political party and sector of Puerto Rican society. *Between Torture and Resistance* presents basic background on the man and his case, and should be read by anyone concerned with aligning U.S. legal practice with international human rights standards and principles.

—Soffiyah Ellijah, executive director, Correctional Association of New York; former deputy director, Harvard Law School Criminal Justice Institute

Martin Luther King Jr. talked about change, defining it as not rolling on the wheels of inevitability but coming through continuous struggle. He also invited us to straighten our backs and work for our freedom. On these pages we will find the story of a man who has dedicated all his life to the struggle for the freedom of his country and, from that commitment, straightened his back with dignity, generosity, and spiritual strength. It is a powerful testimony, born from the cold bars of imprisonment, as a sign of today's injustice and lack of freedom and respect for human rights. *Between Torture and Resistance* is necessary reading for a "reality check" of today's silenced oppression and the profound faith in justice and peace, even in the context of the worst adversities. We know that Oscar, and all of us, will be *free at last.*

—Rev. Angel L. Rivera-Agosto, executive secretary, Puerto Rico Council of Churches

OSCAR LÓPEZ RIVERA

BETWEEN TORTURE AND RESISTANCE

OSCAR LÓPEZ RIVERA

BETWEEN TORTURE AND RESISTANCE

Edited by Luis Nieves Falcón
Foreword by Archbishop Desmond Tutu
Introduction to the English Edition by
Matt Meyer and Rev. Nozomi Ikuta

PM PRESS 2013

Published in cooperation with Resistance in Brooklyn and the Interfaith Prisoners of Conscience Project

Oscar López Rivera: Between Torture and Resistance
Edited by Luis Nieves Falcón

ISBN: 978-1-60486-685-8
LCCN: 2012913622

Cover: John Yates/stealworks.com
Interior: Antumbra Design/antumbradesign.org

10 9 8 7 6 5 4

PM Press
PO Box 23912
Oakland, CA 94623
www.pmpress.org

CONTENTS

PREFACE
Matt Meyer

★

This small book, pieced together from decades of collected letters, commentary, speeches, and leaflets, is a window behind the bars, a squinted look through the blurry bulletproof glass panes of prison visiting rooms. It is the story of a man with a big heart—for his family and for his people. It was put together as a tapestry of sorts by sociologist, educator, lawyer and political-cultural icon Luis Nieves Falcón, whose own life has been a testament to poetic, passionate, strategic, and steadfast commitment to justice, peace, and liberation for the peoples and islands of Puerto Rico. It is a testimony, a biography, and a call to action. It is intended unapologetically to inspire the active engagement of readers: to understand Oscar's motivations and mindset, and to demand his immediate, unconditional release.

After the Foreword and Introductions, which serve as political overviews of the scope and international significance of the man and his "case," the text swings back in time, to a review of

Oscar's life experiences, as narrated by Nieves Falcón-as-editor, putting Oscar's early political life into historical context. As the first chapter takes us from the fields of Vietnam to the streets of Chicago to a decision to go underground, we are led into a short exposition of what clandestinity must have meant for such a vibrant and active leader. The chapter on "court proceedings" that followed Oscar's capture contains quotes from the court record, and the statement penned and spoken by Oscar as part of his reflection on imprisonment. A contribution by noted Puerto Rican poet Carlos Quiles follows.

The remaining three chapters of the book on torture, the nature of life behind bars as constant struggle, and on outlooks for the future are woven together in a rough chronological and thematic order, primarily through excerpts of letters written by and to Oscar, from his brother, sister, daughter, granddaughter, and other close supporters. We have provided exact references to these letters whenever possible and have emphasized the content of those letters rather than the names of their recipients. Oscar and Luis together have crafted the canvas of words and images that bring us to the present. Oscar himself reviewed the final manuscript of this English edition to smooth the edges of a work that is part postcard from prison, part lyrical prose.

In addition, the book was conceived of as a volume to be filled with images: of photos taken in cramped visiting rooms, of the lush colors of Oscar's paintings and portraits, and of Oscar's early life before his imprisonment. Together with the text, they work to bring us closer to the man who has given his life for freedom. Now we must work together, weaving our own art and poetry and political and economic pressures, to ensure that Oscar too may be free.

FOREWORD
Archbishop Desmond M. Tutu, Nobel Peace Laureate

★

When I traveled throughout Africa as a representative of the World Council of Churches in the early 1970s, I witnessed firsthand the ravages of colonialism across diverse lands and conditions; we worked hand-in-hand with those struggling for complete and lasting independence from the indignities of being treated as less than fully human in their own lands. Throughout our struggle in South Africa, it was clear that true freedom meant not just the ability to vote or choose one's own political representatives, but the ability to build one's own schools, to have accessible health care and jobs, to have clean air and water and energy in the control of the communities that utilize them. Of course, true freedom and independence also includes a free and fair judicial system, with responsible and accountable policing, fair legal process, and reasoned judgment and sentencing.

Puerto Rico remains one of the leading territories under direct colonial control, and as such is denied these basic human rights of self-expression. We have watched as students are beaten for wanting an education, bringing back painful memories of South Africa's own history of subjugation and repression. I proudly participated in past calls for a closing of the U.S. military base in Vieques, and freedom for the Puerto Rican political prisoners held behind bars in the United States. We applauded the concessions made in these past campaigns, as prerequisites for a world with greater justice and peace. But one prisoner remains, now a vivid reminder of the ongoing inequality that colonialism and empire building inevitably bring forth. After more than thirty years, Oscar López Rivera is imprisoned for the "crime" of seditious conspiracy: conspiring to free his people from the shackles of imperial injustice.

In March of 2011, I sent a letter about Mr. López Rivera to U.S. President Barack Obama and Attorney General Eric Holder. My Nobel Peace laureate colleagues Mairead Corrigan Maguire of Northern Ireland and Adolfo Pérez Esquivel of Argentina and I expressed our deep concern at that time about the highly irregular and tainted parole hearing that had just taken place. Testimony was permitted at that hearing regarding crimes which López Rivera was never accused of committing in the first place, and a decision was handed down which—in denying parole—pronounced a veritable death sentence by suggesting that no appeal for release be heard again until 2023.

In that 2011 appeal, we noted some compelling aspects of the legal history of this case. "In 1999," we wrote, "President William Jefferson Clinton offered to commute Mr. López Rivera's sentence under the condition that he spend another ten years of good conduct in prison. Because a similar offer was inexplicably denied to another two of Mr. López Rivera's jailed colleagues, he turned that offer down. Now, with more than ten years passed since the original offer, those colleagues—Carlos Alberto Torres and Haydée Beltrán—are both out of jail. Eleven other colleagues, who were released by President Clinton in 1999, have been leading exemplary lives, working in their respective communities to better the lives of their neighbors. Each of us, and many more of our Nobel Prize compatriots, signed petitions at that time and since then which called for the release of all the Puerto Rican political prisoners. Now, we join Javier Jiménez Pérez, the pro-statehood mayor of López Rivera's hometown of San Sebastián, Puerto Rico, and many others across Puerto Rico's political spectrum, in calling for his immediate release."

Between Torture and Resistance now brings the full story of why the release of this one man is so significant. In addition to learning about López Rivera's life as a child in Puerto Rico, as a decorated officer in the U.S. armed services, and as a community organizer in impoverished Puerto Rican neighborhoods, we bear witness to his growth as an artist behind bars. We learn—in his words and his correspondence with beloved Puerto Rican educator, lawyer, and author Luis Nieves Falcón—how López Rivera has kept his faith in sometimes tortuous conditions. In these pages, our own faith and hope can also be renewed.

We must, all of us, understand that there are different kinds of justice in this troubled and beautiful world. Retributive justice is a largely Western concept, and one that we have seen applied unequally based on race and class and other conditions. Our African understanding of justice is far more restorative, with less emphasis on punishment. We believe that we must redress or restore a balance that has been knocked askew. We must work to heal the divisions that have masked the humanness we all share. In any case or interpretation, justice cannot be served by keeping Oscar López Rivera in prison. In working for reconciliation and peace, we once again feel compelled to repeat the Biblical call of Isaiah: to set free those who are bound.

May God bless all of us in our efforts for justice with peace.

INTRODUCTION

Dr. Luis Nieves Falcón

★

In the United States, individual liberties are increasingly being restricted and encroached by the State apparatus, which strives to achieve absolute control of public opinion and annihilate all dissent, while itself generally acting outside the law. Consequently, the State has become the principal threat to individual freedom, the free spirit, and creativity. Basic rights and liberties have become rhetorical for the common citizen, since they have been abjectly robbed of their practical meaning. In fact, the government is characterized by a minimal respect for the law, both domestically and internationally. Basic human rights considerations have been relegated to the lowest possible level of official interest.

In the domestic sphere, the decreasing value of civil rights (those that are vested by law on the individual by government action) is manifested by actions such as these:

- the violation of the right to bail, creating an additional type of punishment by making the magnitude of the bail unreachable for the average citizen;
- the extension of the legal period of incarceration before trial from six months to three years;
- the perversion of the right to freedom from double jeopardy directed at eliminating the use of this defense, particularly when actions of the State are being questioned;
- the imposition of disproportionate sentences;
- the increase in inhuman and degrading prison conditions;
- the increased use of jails and prisons as a principal tool to discourage crime, which has converted the United States into a country with one of the world's highest rates of imprisonment per inhabitant;
- the increase in minors being judged as adult criminals, one of the most disturbing cases being the trial of a six-year-old minor as an adult;
- the persistent imposition of the death penalty; and
- the implementation of anti-immigration policies that are clearly racist in content.

It is not surprising that most of the penal population, including the majority of people sentenced to death and the largest number of children tried as adults, are of black and Hispanic origins. Furthermore, most of the above-named government actions are also racially discriminatory against these people.

Internationally, the United States has shown itself to be a systematic violator of international law. The following are some examples indicative of this conduct:

- illegal intervention in sovereign countries whose economic and political strategies differ from those of the United States;
- the systematic use of the right of exception to evade

compliance with important clauses related to human rights in international agreements;

- withdrawal of acceptance of International Court jurisdiction, after having accepted such, to avoid compliance with adverse decisions;
- refusal by the legal system to accept defenses based on international law, notably in cases where government actions are being questioned;
- the denial of the right to self-determination by territories under the control of the United States that have not yet achieved independence;
- maintaining training facilities for torturers directed at stifling dissent in Third World countries;
- keeping secret prisons in foreign countries, frequently without the knowledge of the country in question, where there are torture centers for dissidents captured elsewhere; and
- open refusal or delay in signing international human rights treaties.

Along with violations of law, the United States has also developed a psychological and emotionally charged campaign to impose upon the population the internalization of a highly negative view of those who are dissidents. This is, in effect, an effort of the State to demonize those who are different, while isolating dissidents from the population at large. In turn, such a campaign seeks to gather support for the illegal conduct of the agencies of the State. The nomenclature used to create these negative categories has changed over time but always retains its high emotional charge.

The original term used to categorize dissidence was "seditious individual," a legal term which arose during the U.S. Civil War and that was applied exclusively to individuals from the Southern states who favored secession. The term remained dormant after the conflict ended, until 1937 when antisedition legislation was invoked against the Nationalist Party of Puerto Rico and its leadership in order to justify their imprisonment and thereby diminish opposition to the U.S. regime in Puerto Rico and growing support for independence. The Nationalist leadership was accused of conspiring to overthrow by force U.S. legal authority over Puerto Rico. Since then, antiseditious legislation in the United States has been almost exclusively reserved to attack Puerto Ricans who favor independence.

At the end of the Second World War, and during the so-called "Cold War," the term of choice became "subversive." The U.S. government made a conscious and systematic effort to associate dissent within the country and its territories with international communism. Thus, the category of "subversive" became synonymous with "communist."

At the end of the "Cold War," when the term "communist" lost credibility as an element of social policy, the term "terrorist" emerged. It is interesting that the ideological-emotional-deprecatory content of the category remains immutable: forces of evil that operate domestically, but under external influences for the sole purpose of subverting and destroying the democratic value system. As with the previous designations, the people who are branded with the new epithet become the main suspects for all "crimes"; they are labor leaders, academics, youth, and *independentistas.*

Now it is emphasized that these people cannot be expected to be neutralized as a group, they are not candidates for rehabilitation, and it is strongly recommended that they be permanently separated from society or annihilated. High-ranking officials of the Federal Bureau of Investigation (FBI) concluded in regard to this situation, "Only one side can truly survive. If the terrorist cannot be neutralized, nothing less than the death of a terrorist will keep him from repeating his act."[1]

Given this ideological foundation, the imprisonment of a dissident is seen as a transitional step in the process of his or her physical elimination. The behavior control units, behavior modification chambers, and the emphasis on prolonged isolation that have arisen in U.S. prisons are in line with this purpose, since

---

[1] John Brown Anti-Klan Committee, *Repression: Documents from the FBI, Think Tanks, and Other Repressive Agencies* (Chicago: Rebeldia Publications, 1983).

according to the advisers of the prison authorities, this isolation provokes the loss of mental faculties, the nervous system is permanently damaged, and drives them to suicide.[2]

The rise in violations of civil and human rights by the State results in different levels of resistance against specific domestic and foreign policies, which in turn leads to a public policy of cruel and vengeful repression. The ultimate goal is to eliminate dissent by all means that are available to the repressive apparatus of the State.

In the conflict arising from the illegal conduct of the State—which includes, but is not limited to crimes against peace and against humanity as well as war crimes—and the resistance by an opposition that combats the illegal actions of the State, the judicial system is revealed as an important partner in the official strategy of repression. In fact, the judicial system frequently becomes a public collaborator with this authoritarian and despotic government. The system has sanctioned official policies directed against Third World peoples and European-Americans within U.S. society who have dared to raise their voices in protest. All illegal conduct of the State is sanctioned; all vindicatory actions taken by resisters are criminalized. The absolute power of the former and the total vulnerability of the latter become increasingly apparent.

The struggle between preserving and eroding existing civil and human rights accentuates the characteristics of the parties in the judicial arena: those of the magistrate—who assumes the role of prosecutor besides that of a judge—and those of the accused.

Judicial discourse has a common ideological content: the obstinate refusal to accept that in the United States there are people who are persecuted and imprisoned for holding ethical and political positions that are in opposition to those sustained by the U.S. government; the furious denial of the existence of political prisoners in U.S. jails and prisons; the assertion that the only avenues open to dissidents are the electoral process and official channels of expression; the denial that revolutionary actions

[2] Department of Justice, Law Enforcement Assistance Administration, "Memorandum of July 26, 1978," 1.

are a legitimate avenue of change; the use of linguistic categories of a deprecatory nature to classify dissidents and thereby justify disproportionate sentences, which allow for the permanent removal from society of dissidents and political militants, while at the same time allowing criminal violators of international law to walk about freely and with impunity.

The use of the sentencing process to add to the verdict (as a retaliation against the dissident's refusal to submit to the forced legitimizing of the authority and illegal actions of the State), and the use of the death penalty or equivalent sentences, serve as a dissuasive measure for any future political action. Finally, this judicial discourse reflects a systematic refusal of any defense based on international law, obviously because international law recognizes the rights of citizens to resist any government that violates basic human rights.

The profile that emerges of this legal discourse also shows support for the State in its efforts to conceal its violations of law, a discourse that serves the interests of an authoritarian and despotic structure. This profile clearly reveals that the voices of dissent are seen as a threat to the prevailing oppressive structure in which the judicial system plays an important part. These are shared interests which both will defend to the death. This is why the judicial branch has no qualms in publicly endorsing the illegal actions of the government and its abuse against the voices of the opposition.

The other profile, that of the resisters and militants who have been imprisoned for their objections of conscience, is a profile of a group of people who are deeply committed to fighting against racism and social injustice and growing militarization and nuclearization. They fight against: U.S. collaboration with racist regimes; military interventions in sovereign states; the continuing aid the United States gives to dictatorial regimes; U.S. participation in terrible atrocities against peoples who are engaged in liberation struggles; and the continued imposition of a colonial regime in Puerto Rico. All of these official actions involve violations of international law, the compliance of which are compulsory for U.S. citizens as established in the Nuremberg principles. In the case of the Puerto Rican political prisoners in particular, their conduct with regard to the colonial domination of their country is protected by international law, which allows victims of colonialism to use whatever means that may be available to them to overcome this crime against all of humanity. International law also requires that all citizens of the United States come to the aid of the aggrieved party, the People of Puerto Rico, or face individual accountability just as the German people had to answer for the crimes of Nazism.

The forces that control the power structure in the United States feel threatened by principled people and continue with their vengeful behavior against them in the *gulag* of the U.S. prison system. The long list of abuses against these prisoners is so extensive that international standards of treatment of prisoners are violated systematically in a sadistic manner with regard to Puerto Rican political prisoners. Besides Oscar—some of whose experiences, including his twelve years of absolute isolation, are recounted more fully here—one was subjected to four strip searches before a legal visit and four more after the visit, and one of the women was held in an underground behavior modification chamber for three years.

This is how a person who once was a political prisoner explains what it means to be a Puerto Rican political prisoner:

> They tied me with invisible ropes
> And shackles of lead
>
> They drained the blood from my veins
> They spat in my face
>
> On the hour sharp
> They put me in a green box
> They broke my throat
> So that I couldn't sing
>
> So that I could not speak the truths
> Of my blood-soaked homeland
>
> On the hour sharp
> They blindfolded my eyes

To darken the light of my gaze

That kept speaking the truths
And speaking of my trampled land . . .

They shut me in in a bitter cell
And broke down my life bit by bit

On the hour sharp
And once more they left me alone

In that bitter cell

They went off, one by one, step by step
They went off, defeated and straggling

Finally, understanding
That they had imprisoned a man, but not the Homeland

On the hour sharp.

—Humberto Pagán Hernández
Desde la Cárcel (from prison), 1973

What are the charges raised by Puerto Rican political prisoners against the United States? What are the actions of the United States in their homeland—Puerto Rico—that they are resisting?

- The colonial domination that the U.S. government has exercised over Puerto Rico for more than a hundred years.

- The U.S. government's refusal during the last three decades to comply with a resolution of the United Nations Decolonization Committee recognizing Puerto Rico's right to free self-determination and independence. The Committee's injunction for the United States to initiate the process that would allow Puerto Rico to exercise this right has been ignored. This refusal by the United States violates the right to free self-determination as expressed in the United Nations Charter as well as in the treaties on economic and social rights and civil and political rights.

- The political and economic domination of Puerto Rico by the United States that has been characterized by a systematic and persistent strategy of cultural assimilation. In this strategy, the language and culture of Puerto Rico are constantly besieged and their healthy and autonomous development is prevented. This conduct of the United States violates Article 27 of the International Covenant on Civil and Political Rights: the right of a people to fully enjoy its culture and its language.

- The United States consistently has imposed on Puerto Rico a model of economic dependence that violates Article 1.2 of the International Covenant on economic, social, and cultural rights, which guarantees "All peoples may, for their own ends, freely dispose of their natural wealth and resources. . . . In no case may a people be deprived of its own means of subsistence."

- Puerto Ricans who oppose the political and economic subordination of their country, those who support the right to free self-determination and those who sympathize with or openly defend the right of Puerto Rico to independence are subject to systematic of repression and criminalization by U.S. authorities. They are considered guilty of unspecified crimes, regardless of whether they have engaged in conduct that is considered to be illegal. Police dossiers have been prepared on people simply for being *independentistas,* and *independentistas* have been fired from their jobs in Puerto Rico's public sector for their beliefs and ideals. This conduct is shameful, given that neither defending independence nor fighting against colonialism is a crime. The actions of the United States in this regard constitute a violation of Articles 2 and 15 of the International Declaration of Human Rights and the International Covenant on civil and political rights, respectively, which guarantee that "No one shall be held guilty of any criminal offence on account of any act or omission which did not constitute a criminal offence under national or international law"; and violation of Articles 18 and 19 of the above documents which guarantee that "Everyone shall have the right to hold opinions without interference. . . . Everyone shall have the right to freedom of expression" and, furthermore, "this right shall include freedom to seek, receive and impart information and ideas of all kinds, regardless of frontiers."

- The strategy of repression against Puerto Ricans who favor independence also violates the right to freedom of assembly and peaceful association; the right of all persons to be free from arbitrary interference of privacy, their families, their homes, and their reputations; the right to equal access to public service in their country; and, finally, the right of all people to work.

- The obstinate refusal by the United States to apply the UN General Assembly resolution on colonialism in Puerto Rico and the treatment that captured anticolonial combatants receive.[3] This illegal conduct not only ignores international law, it categorizes dissidents and combatants as terrorists. There is no question that this conduct of the U.S. government is a clear effort to conceal its own tactics of terror against the people of Puerto Rico, while at the same time justifying its own violations of the minimum standards for the treatment of prisoners.

There is no question that not even a drop of generosity is to be expected from that despotic oppressor. Both in the case of our former political prisoners and in the case of Oscar López Rivera, we are certain that the ultimate purpose is to prevent these men and women from assuming the long-standing tradition of revolutionary struggle in Puerto Rico to break down the existing repressive and authoritarian structure.

---

[3] Resolution 2621 (XXV), October 12, 1970, and Resolution 3103 (XXVIII), December 12, 1973.

Here and now, on this side of the jail and prison bars, we all share a moral duty and obligation. We must multiply the struggle; transform the struggle so that it will reach everywhere. From our neighborhood blocks and meeting places to the halls of official activity, we need to fight for Oscar, who has been imprisoned for thirty years in many U.S. jails and prisons because his struggle on behalf of Puerto Rico is also on behalf of us all. The struggle for freedom in any corner of the globe is the struggle for the freedom of all. We must fight to eradicate the demonizing stereotypes that the oppressors have constructed around this brave opponent.

We have to multiply the struggle because it is the only way that we can raise an ever-growing voice, a stentorian, booming voice, in favor of Oscar, who is confined in these bitter cells just for being a person of principle. We have to multiply the struggle to ensure that Oscar López Rivera is freed.

We must step up the struggle to let the world know the situation of subjection in which he has been placed, which in the end is our own condition of subjection.

We have to multiply the struggle to ensure his freedom, which is also our own freedom. We have to intensify the struggle with our actions, reaffirming that peace and love are the essential principle of a liberated humanity in a new life of fraternal solidarity.

We are going to struggle, because the struggle is only the beginning of a national and international outcry against the terrible conditions that have been imposed on this warrior against colonialism in the allegedly democratic society of the United States.

Our awareness in solidarity of this oppression that touches us all is the starting point of a new and necessary impetus for the struggle. . . . because only struggle will make us free. This is what is revealed to us by the patriot who refuses to bow down under the yoke of oppression.

INTRODUCTION TO THE ENGLISH EDITION

Matt Meyer and Rev. Nozomi Ikuta

★

The U.S. inserts itself into Puerto Rican life on an almost daily basis, disingenuously posing as "the knight in shining armor." As one pro-statehood proponent recognized, "Every part of the colonial, economic, and juridical life of Puerto Ricans is regulated by the federal government: There is no human activity in Puerto Rico that isn't covered by some federal agency."[1] Yet that pervasive presence is ever-expanding . . .

The U.S. president greeted Burma's decision to release hundreds of political prisoners as "a crucial step

[1] Hernán Padilla, "La federalización de Puerto Rico," *El Nuevo Día*, November 14, 2011, http://www.elnuevodia.com/columna-lafederalizaciondepuertorico-1118618.html.

in Burma's democratic transformation and national reconciliation process" and "urge[d] the government to . . . free all remaining prisoners of conscience."[2] During her visit to Burma, and after meeting with a celebrated political prisoner, U.S. Secretary of State Clinton was widely quoted as saying, "We believe that any political prisoner anywhere should be released," and that "One political prisoner is one too many in our view."

There should be no problem, then, with President Obama's compliance with [the United Nations Decolonization] Committee's resolution to release the valiant Puerto Rican independentistas in U.S. custody, so that perhaps next year Oscar López Rivera can stand at the side of his compañeros and speak in support of independence for his homeland.

—Jan Susler, National Lawyers Guild International Committee Presentation to the United Nations Decolonization Committee Hearings on Puerto Rico (excerpt), June 18, 2012[3]

An entire generation has been born and come of age since Oscar López Rivera was arrested on May 29, 1981. For many North Americans, the intervening decades have let the movements for civil rights and against the war in Vietnam fade into minor footnotes in our historical memory. The election of an African American president in 2008 led many people to imagine that "the color line" articulated by W.E.B. Du Bois a century ago had been eradicated. A simple look at prison statistics, however—such as the fact spotlighted in Michelle Alexander's *The New Jim Crow* that today more males of African descent are currently behind bars than were enslaved in the years prior to the Civil War—suggests that the glaring divide between Black and White America cannot be ignored.

---

[2] President Barack Obama, "Release of Burmese Political Prisoners," January 13, 2012, http://www.humanrights.gov/2012/01/13/release-of-burmese-political-prisoners-statement-by-president-obama/.

[3] National Lawyers Guild International Committee, http://www.nlginternational.org/news/article.php?nid=486.

In 1992, as the world commemorated the five-hundredth anniversary of the "encounter" between European adventurers and the Indigenous nation-builders of the so-called New World, the United Nations called for a process to end to all colonialism. As one of the planet's last "non-self-governing territories" and direct colony of the United States, Puerto Rico's status was a significant focus of much of the quincentenary's political work. In the primer *Puerto Rico: The Cost of Colonialism* produced by the Fellowship of Reconciliation, we raised the question of why modern-day North American peace activists should focus special attention on the Caribbean island under U.S. imperial control.

Given the wealth of solidarity offered to other struggles, we wrote, why not develop massive and mainstream progressive support "for the Latin American nation that, along with Mexico, is interwoven into the very fabric of U.S. life and history?" With over four million Puerto Ricans living "stateside" in the United States (since 2003 possibly exceeding the number of Puerto Ricans living on their island), there is a special responsibility inherent among human rights advocates of the north to understand deeply the justice issues of this "community" which is in reality a nation. Any quick or careful review of Puerto Rico, or of the Puerto Rican diaspora in the United States will show poor socioeconomic status, few educational or vocational choices, and a legal system dependent on the use of English only on the "federal" court level. Throughout the twentieth century, Puerto Ricans were drafted into the U.S. Armed Forces and sent to the front lines of wars in Europe and Asia—all while ineligible and unable to vote for the U.S. president and commander-in-chief who would determine their fate.

Yet solidarity among North American progressives for our Puerto Rican brothers and sisters has not been a priority for much of the hundred-plus years since U.S. Marines landed in San Juan in 1898. Those who continue to make up our country's imperial subjects know well the indignities of colonial oppression—and also know well that there are still many who, in the words of Congressman Luis V. Gutiérrez, take a "firm stance on the need to affirm Puerto Rican identity and the existence of a Puerto Rican nation." Despite divisions within the Puerto Rican population on how best to assert their political options vis-à-vis the United States, there can be little doubt that no sovereignty currently exists. When the Catholic Archbishop of San Juan, Roberto González Nieves, asserts that "motherland, nation and identity are indivisible gifts of God's love," the struggle for self-determination, unfettered by policies set forth by U.S. courtrooms or Congress, must be clear.

One directive on decolonization set forth by the United Nations and enshrined in the Universal Declaration of Human Rights is the freedom from imprisonment based on political beliefs or positions. "Seditious conspiracy"—the thought-crime of discussing with one's closest colleagues the need to display discontent against the established order—is a particularly dubious label to justify decades behind bars. Political prisoners, in particular, are to be released according to UN protocol before any process of self-determination is to be internationally recognized and accepted. When Presidents Carter and Clinton each provided amnesty or clemency for Puerto Rican political prisoners, it was based on Puerto Rican and international pressures regarding these well-established rights. That political prisoner Oscar López Rivera still languishes in U.S. jails, facing torturous conditions since 1981, is a disgrace to the very notion of "the land of the free." Oscar remains in prison long after all of his associates have been released (all of whom play productive, nonviolent roles constructing and contributing to the communities where they live), a model prisoner denied parole because of vengeful not rehabilitative purposes. If the U.S. government followed the international rules and regulations regarding prison conditions and procedures which it has agreed to, or the anticolonial legacy which it rhetorically makes reference to, Oscar López Rivera would have been set free long ago.

For us, as professionals who have stood in solidarity and friendship with Oscar and with the people of Puerto Rico for many years, the moral is clear: we have much to learn from and gain in our relationships with those unjustly persecuted. We ourselves grow, in humility and humanity, as we work to help others live lives of freedom and emancipation. We ourselves benefit, in our personal and political insights, as we are taught the true meaning of courage and creative resistance to wrong-doing. It is therefore an act of profound gratefulness, a true labor of love, to help with bringing about this English-language edition of Oscar López Rivera's new book, expertly crafted in association with Dr. Luis Nieves Falcón.

It is always harder to deal with the oppression that is close to home than the one at a faraway "safe" distance. As the recent reflection on "Solidarity and Its Discontents" written by the Raha Iranian Feminist Collective so beautifully articulates, a "crucial imperative of solidarity" is "the ability to understand the context of other people's struggles, to stand in their shoes." In a period where there is more than one source of global oppression, or even imperialism, a concrete and effective solidarity "from below" must include differently articulated aspirations of mass movements against colonialism, neocolonialism, and recolonization; state and collective militarism; dictatorship; economic crisis; gender, sexual, religious, class, and ethnic oppression. With greater emphasis on defining and deepening solidarity as a form of multinational social struggle against dominant transnational paradigms (as in popular view throughout the Occupy movements and in David Featherstone's and others' recent academic work), our own examples of solidarity must be strengthened and sharpened. Solidarity must not be about charity or pity but, as Mozambican founding president Samora Machel pointed out, must be based upon a mutual understanding of two peoples striking a single blow against a common enemy.

We hope that this book, reflecting for new audiences the words and life of Puerto Rican patriot Oscar López Rivera, can be one blow against the degrading practice of valuing some people's lives over others. When the original Spanish-language edition appeared in Puerto Rico late in 2011, we knew that a revised English edition was needed to bring information about Oscar's case, as well as his indomitable spirit of resistance to a wider solidarity audience.

As Oscar has shown in his "artistic" example of steady, soft-spoken determination, sticking to his people's goals of freedom as Nelson Mandela did before him, victories are not won overnight but require constant vigilance. They require individual acts of the heart and broad international campaigns. We hope that this book will help each reader to join us in working for Oscar's freedom, or to redouble your efforts to see that all political prisoners and those wrongly accused are released.

We hope that the beauty of Oscar's life, art, and work will inspire all of us to greater encounters—ones on equal footings with justice and peace as our goals—to unite for a solidarity which will include the whole world.

LIFE EXPERIENCES: 1943–1976

★

. . . i can go to bed every night with a clean conscience because there is no blood on my hands, and because my heart remains full of love and compassion.[1]

i was born Boricua, i will keep being Boricua, and will die a Boricua.[2] i refuse to accept injustice, and will never ignore it when i become aware of it. If i can't do good to someone, at least i will never do them harm. And if i have nothing good to say about someone, i'll say nothing at all.

i have never left anybody behind. The alleged victims said that if the Parole Commission had informed

---

[1] Except for the court proceedings excerpted in chapters 3 and 4 and the letter in the final chapter, Oscar does not capitalize the "i" when referring to himself, in order to deemphasize the individual with respect to the collective.

[2] A Puerto Rican, based on *Borikén*, the indigenous name for the island.

> them that Carlos was applying for parole they would have never allowed it and he would have had to rot in jail.[3] We can celebrate that i am the only one left. The compa' is already making and rebuilding his life, and things are going very well for him.[4]
>
> Well, take good care of yourself, don't neglect your health, and pa'lante always with hope and courage.[5] Lots and lots of love,
>
> —Oscar López Rivera, letter to his daughter Clarisa, February 2, 2011

Oscar López Rivera was born under the sign of Capricorn, on January 6, 1943, in Barrio Aibonito of San Sebastián, Puerto Rico.

His parents were Doña Ana Rivera Méndez ("Mita") and Don Alberto López Méndez. The family is made up of six children of both parents, plus three children of Don Alberto, and one foster child. They are, in order of age: Juan Alberto (resident of Isabela), Clara Luz (deceased), Mercedes (resident of Aguada), Oscar (imprisoned), José (resident of Chicago), and Zenaida (resident of Chicago). The foster son, Hilario Medina and the three children of Don Alberto—Carlos, Iván, and Maricely—are residents of San Sebastián.

Oscar went to elementary school in Escuela Guerrero of Barrio Aibonito, and attended Escuela Hoyamala in Barrio Hoyamala for the first years of middle school. He spent those formative years—in which the values that shelter our spirit are developed—in the rural countryside, which instilled in him a profound love of the homeland and its core values: a life full of primary relationships characterized by the tenderness and affection that are distinguishing traits typical of Puerto Rican family attachment bonds.

Because of the precarious situation of the country, Oscar's family joined the thousands of Puerto Ricans who, as in the

---

[3] Carlos Alberto Torres, Oscar's friend and fellow political prisoner, released in 2010.

[4] Short for *compañero*, friend, companion, partner, comrade.

[5] Short for *para adelante*, a term of encouragement meaning "go forward" or "onward."

poem "The Peasant of Las Marias," found themselves obliged to abandon their native soil in the hope of improving their economic situation.[6] His father, a small farmer, was forced to emigrate in 1952 and headed for Chicago where his wife's two brothers lived, leaving the entire family behind. Don Alberto worked in a steel mill, where he suffered a work accident, losing partial use of his right hand. As settlement of the resulting suit, he was made a supervisor and received some economic compensation. In 1957, Clara and her husband followed the route of emigration. Their older brother, Juan Alberto, joined them in 1958, followed immediately by the rest of the family. Oscar left the Island when he was fourteen.

Oscar finished high school in Chicago in 1960 and began liberal arts studies at Wright College in Chicago in 1961. He was fascinated by the sciences, especially biology and mathematics. Many years later, while in jail, he reencountered this love of plants and now often paints leaves as a representation of liberating hope.

The leap to Chicago was hard. Mita explains it like this: "My husband came looking for a better environment and it was not to be found here. We have to work harder, it's colder, [there is] more humiliation, more racism for us. . . . We live humiliated by the Americans. If you go to work in a factory, they fire you because 'you don't produce.' That applies to Hispanics, Blacks, not for Americans. We Latinos all suffer. We suffer in this country."[7]

In Chicago, the family situation became critical. The authoritarian, womanizing father from Barrio Aibonito forced Mercedes to work in a factory when she refused to be dropped back a grade because she came from Puerto Rico. Mercedes eventually married, and gave birth to two children, Fabián and Wanda. Mercedes's husband, however, had an accident that resulted in the partial amputation of his leg, and turned him into a short-tempered man, angry at the world at large. After

---

[6] A poem by Puerto Rican poet laureate Juan Antonio Corretjer.

[7] Miñi Seijo Bruno, "Los once prisioneros de guerra 'Son pobres y puertorriqueños.'" *Claridad*, February 27–March 5, 1981.

he became abusive toward Mercedes, they separated and had no further relationship.

Don Alberto also decided to abandon the family and disappeared completely. Oscar left his studies to help support the family. Between 1962 and 1963, he worked in a medical laboratory and from 1963–1965 for GTE (General Telephone and Electronics) in Northlake, Illinois. He was drafted in June 1965. In the front lines of Vietnam, Oscar learned the horrors of war firsthand.

Oscar risked his life in Vietnam to save his comrades and was awarded the Bronze Star for meritorious service. His time there also awakened previously unexperienced feelings about Puerto Rico.

First, the Puerto Rican flag became a symbol of important unity among the Puerto Rican soldiers. Recognizing the familiar common colors filled war-tormented soldiers with overwhelming pride and the flag became a physical symbol of powerful emotions. The soldiers may have left the Homeland behind in body, but they remained firmly attached to it in spirit.

Second, Oscar began to question his role in such a terrible war. Why did they have to kill people who had done nothing to them? Why kill people who appeared to have things in common with Puerto Ricans themselves? He began to question the actions of North American imperialism in that Southeast Asian country, and the role of Puerto Ricans in the imperialist wars of the United States. These two seeds—cultural nationalism and anticolonial struggle—begin to germinate in Oscar's mind in Vietnam, and ripened later in his life.

When the horror of his involvement in the war in came to an end, Oscar returned to Chicago. He began studies at Roosevelt University but did not finish them. He was deeply troubled by the conditions of life faced by Puerto Ricans and other ethnic minorities in the city, horrified by the destruction of youth by drugs, and by the subhuman conditions in which the majority of his compatriots lived. In 1968, he began to do community work with the Northwest Community Organization (NCO).

The NCO based its work in the thinking of Saul Alinsky, who, during the 1930s, developed a movement that advocated the principle that poor people could gain power by organizing their strongest sectors. In that organization, Oscar came into contact with two of Alinsky's disciples—Shel Trapp and Gayle Cincotta—who greatly influenced him and contributed to developing his thinking about community work.

His commitment to community struggles grew. Between 1969 and 1970, he also began a relationship with Justina Ramos, whom he had met many years before. His only daughter, Clarisa, was born to them in 1971. Oscar's fervor in favor of his people intensified and he was deeply dedicated to a broad range of causes between 1969 and 1976.

Access to education for Puerto Ricans and other ethnic groups suffering discrimination claimed Oscar's immediate attention. In 1972, Oscar helped found the Pedro Albizu Campos High School (PACHS) to assure the best possible education for students in the community through an alternative school controlled by Puerto Ricans themselves. Oscar articulated a powerful vision of how alternative schools can challenge the essentially racist system of mainstream U.S. education. After PACHS was formed, Oscar called for a gathering of eight alternative schools in the Chicago area to organize for a democratizing impact on state education. In this effort to expand educational horizons for the entire city, celebrated Brazilian educational innovator Paulo Freire, author of *Pedagogy of the Oppressed*, was invited to share his experiences of liberatory models of education.

In 1973, Oscar helped found the Juan Antonio Corretjer Puerto Rican Cultural Center (PRCC), which to this day works closely with the still-thriving PACHS. The PRCC became a center for the promotion of cultural persistence and resistance for the Puerto Rican population and its rich cultural heritage. Through the PRCC, Puerto Ricans have been able to preserve their dignity as people while heightening their appreciation of their own culture.

Oscar also joined the struggle for bilingual education in Wells High School and Tuley High School (later known as Roberto Clemente High School), which served the Puerto Rican population of Chicago. Through doing so, Oscar met others who would later be his comrades in political organizations for Puerto Rican independence. They won a minor victory with the approval of a Transitional Bilingual Education Law in 1973, establishing the first bilingual program at the José de Diego School in Chicago, where it survives to this day.

Even with these reforms, Oscar understood that the inclusion of bilingualism in the education of Puerto Ricans and Latinos would not be enough for real community improvement. He understood that access to institutions of higher education was necessary to improve the economic and social situation of these populations and chose the two public state universities—the University of Illinois and Northeastern Illinois University—as the targets of the next series of actions. The intense struggle to improve poor people's access to public universities involved protests and police brutality, continued protests and arrests. These efforts, part of the greater upsurge of protest and struggle throughout the country, led to the establishment of Project 500 at the University of Illinois, an educational initiative to ensure the annual admission of five hundred Latino and African American students.

The newly established Latin American and Latino studies and Proyecto Pa'lante at introduced curricula relating to Latinos in the Chicago diaspora and Latin American cultural and political studies of the respective countries from which the Chicago diaspora originated to the Northeastern Illinois University. Oscar's participation in this work was rooted in the belief that every person has a fundamental right to enjoy his or her own culture, and to avoid the cultural erosion produced by forced assimilation into the dominant Anglo-Saxon one.

Oscar's efforts also helped to create the Latin American Recruitment Education Service (LARES) program, also still in existence. Lares is a Puerto Rican town known for its historic nineteenth-century uprising against Spanish colonialism, and the LARES program is an intellectual effort to contribute to the persisting presence of liberation ideals in Chicago's education system.

In 1975, Oscar helped establish the first Latino Cultural Center in the state of Illinois. Named after educator Rafael Cintrón-Ortiz, the center recognizes and honors an admired professor at the University of Illinois, who was brought to Chicago from Puerto Rico to teach the history of the island.

Along with the struggles for educational reform, Oscar also helped increase employment opportunities and improve working conditions for the Puerto Rican population. Oscar and the other organizers in the Spanish Coalition for Jobs built coalitions within the Latino community to challenge the discriminatory practices of the construction and utilities industries and organized demonstrations at different construction sites, including Roberto Clemente High School, to disrupt the construction process. Massive demonstrations organized by the Spanish Coalition for Jobs also forced Illinois Bell to hire Latinos and open offices to serve the Latino community.

In the same spirit, Oscar also helped organize the Spanish Coalition for Housing to improve housing conditions for Puerto Ricans and free them from the rat- and cockroach-infested basements in which many were living. This involved direct confrontation with the (often absentee) landlords who collected excessive rents while pocketing the money and refusing to make the pigsties they rented to Puerto Ricans even remotely inhabitable. Protests in luxurious neighborhoods, in front of the homes of the exploitative landlords, acquired a dramatic character when rats and cockroaches "collected" from the apartments the landlords refused to clean up were released in front of the landlords' own mansions.

During this critical period, Oscar also participated in the movements to improve hospital conditions and medical services for the most disenfranchised groups of the city. His civil activism between 1969 and 1976 clearly evidenced his genuine and significant effort to use every possible route of change within Chicago's existing official structures. The question, however, remained: was it really possible to develop lasting (and not merely cosmetic) change within the prevailing dominant structures of U.S. society?

Throughout his civic involvement, Oscar had not yet developed a definitive consciousness or position in favor of independence for Puerto Rico, but a number of historic episodes during that time moved him in the direction of supporting independence.

In 1950, the Nationalist Party of Puerto Rico founded a Nationalist Board in Chicago. The group organized readings and discussions around the writings of Doña Laura Albizu

Meneses about her husband, renowned Nationalist Party President and political prisoner Pedro Albizu Campos. Oscar was one of a group of young people who moved by what he read about Campos and his life.

On June 12, 1966 (while Oscar was still in Vietnam), the "Division Street riots" took place in Chicago after the Knights of Columbus organized the city's first Puerto Rican parade in a downtown area traditionally reserved for the national festivities of white groups. After the parade, they returned to celebrate in Humboldt Park, part of the Puerto Rican neighborhood. During a brawl in a Puerto Rican bar, the police came in and killed a young Puerto Rican. The enraged crowd carried the youth, on foot, to the hospital and riots erupted for three days.

Martin Luther King Jr., who visited Chicago in 1966, declared it one of the most racist cities in the United States. In 1967, the Young Lords, a Chicago street gang, transformed itself into a political movement that publicly advocated for the independence of Puerto Rico. Although Oscar did not belong to the organization, he participated in some of its activities. In the same year, a "Red Squad" was created within the Chicago Police Department, dedicated to infiltrating and repressing progressive organizations, including Hispanic ones.

In 1973, in the midst of intense and varied campaigns and movements, Oscar was invited to join the National Hispanic Commission of the Episcopal Church. He and others in the Commission advocated on behalf of the Nationalist prisoners, a group of *independentistas* who had attacked the U.S. Congress in 1954 and Blair House in 1950.[8] He also worked with indigenous peoples, Chicanos, and Puerto Ricans across the United States.

Between his experiences in Vietnam and his civic activism home, Oscar began to develop a more radical ideological posi-

---

[8] Oscar Collazo attacked Blair House, the temporary residence of the president, in 1950. Lolita Lebrón, Rafael Cancel Miranda, Andrés Figueroa Cordero, and Irving Flores Rodríguez attacked the U.S. Congress in 1954 to call attention to the "Commonwealth" Constitution, which led to the removal of Puerto Rico from the UN list of non-self-governing territories. After twenty-five years in prison, the Nationalist prisoners were pardoned by President Carter in 1979.

tion regarding Puerto Rico. At this time, an underground organization—the Armed Forces of National Liberation (FALN)—carried out various bombings and militant actions in the United States. Grand Jury investigations, "fishing" for information about the group, were held both in 1974 and in 1976–1977. As a result of these investigations, several members of the National Hispanic Commission of the Episcopal Church of New York and Chicago (including Oscar's brother José), were jailed for refusing to cooperate with the Grand Jury in a principled stance against cooperation with colonizing authorities as modeled by Albizu Campos.

TIME UNDERGROUND: 1976–1981

★

The Grand Jury's "fishing expeditions" added a level of repression to an already tense situation, and Oscar—as a well-known community leader—was a clear target. Under the threat of immediate arrest by the FBI, Oscar and his three closest comrades in the struggle chose to go underground to continue their political action in secret, at the fringe of civil society. With this action, they joined a long tradition of clandestine political action dating back two thousand years from the early days of Christianity, through the much-celebrated Underground Railroad, right up to modern times.

The decision was necessary but more painful than they had anticipated as an abstract possibility now turned into a harsh and often frightful reality. Nevertheless, a brave person acts with determination despite misgivings and fear, and must resist panic at all costs. Oscar's experience in Vietnam had revealed to him that utter desperation could ward off fear. It took the four comrades who opted to go underground two months of constant movement before they could meet again and support one another.

The new way of life in hiding meant no steady home. Not being able to enjoy the day-to-day things that give us pleasure. Not being able to smell a flower without fear about who is watching. Not being able to contemplate the calm of the ocean—that extensive blue ocean which surrounds Puerto Rico. Not being able to share experiences with our beautiful people, with family, with comrades. It means, as well, to discover the hidden brutality of the oppressor—one's own bestializing.

The situation required breaking all family ties and contact with loved ones. Ignoring this reality would not only have put loved ones in danger but also put at risk the liberty of those underground. However, the most painful part of clandestine life was knowing that family members were being harassed, and not to be able to do anything about it. The FBI unleashed a chain of persecution upon those closest to the revolutionaries: they threatened family members with death, invaded their homes, ambushed them and questioned them at gunpoint, physically assaulted them and held them accountable for actions they knew nothing about. The absolute support by family members, despite the browbeating treatment, is testimony to their valor and intense love.

Oscar remained underground from November 1976 until his capture in 1981. Then began the false process of a "fair trial" and the torture of imprisonment.

COURT PROCEEDINGS

Defendant: Oscar López Rivera

Charge: Seditious conspiracy: To conspire to overthrow by force the authority of the United States over Puerto Rico

Sentence: 55 years

Judge: Hon. McMillen: "If I could I would sentence them to the electric chair."[1]

Lead Prosecutor: Jeremy Margolis: "I would like to see these Puerto Ricans die in jail."[2]

---

[1] Court Record, page 649, from trial of Oscar's eleven comrades arrested in Evanston, Illinois, on April 4, 1980. The same judge and prosecutor were involved in Oscar's trial in 1981.

[2] Ibid., 34.

Statement by Oscar López Rivera:

Given my revolutionary principles, the legacy of our heroic freedom fighters, and my respect for international law—the only law which has a right to judge my actions—it is my obligation and my duty to declare myself a prisoner of war. I therefore do not recognize the jurisdiction of the United States government over Puerto Rico or of this court to try me or judge me.

This very proceeding is illegal because it violates international law and my rights as a prisoner of war. Bearing in mind that I am accused of seditious conspiracy, of using force to oppose the authority of the United States, the political nature of this process further guarantees the illegality and injustice of this proceeding. Further, this is not a trial, not even a kangaroo court. It is just a ritual, a formality, because Judge McMillen, Jeremy Margolis, the FBI, and all the people who represent them have already tried me and found me guilty in absentia. Since my capture, the FBI has circulated a memorandum describing me as a dangerous person and a terrorist.

I consider it also my duty and obligation to explain and to clarify the historical reasons and the basis for assuming the position of prisoner of war. I want everyone to be clear and conscious regarding our struggle and the truly colonial case of Puerto Rico, so that they cannot claim ignorance when history and justice reckon with them, including Judge McMillen, Jeremy Margolis, the FBI, and everyone who represents the interests of the government of the United States.

In the following statement, I intend to discuss five important questions which demonstrate that Puerto Rico is a colony and that I have every right to fight for the freedom of my country and to be treated as a prisoner of war. These are: (1) Puerto Rico is a territory maintained in captivity as a result of a previous military conquest; (2) the population of Puerto Rico has been subjected to the colonial rule of the United States; (3) the United States has pursued a policy of genocide and extermination, denying us the most fundamental rights of life and liberty; (4) there is a geographical, psychological, cultural, religious, linguistic and spiritual divide between Puerto Rico and the United States; (5) the colonial elections held in Puerto Rico are illegitimate given that truly democratic elections can only take place when the colonizing nation returns full sovereignty to the colony. These five points are the central basis and foundation for the POW position which I am assuming here today.[3]

I wish to add a simple additional remark. Mr. Margolis has said that there are democratic ways to struggle and get things done. He forgets to tell you that I have a history of precisely that. That I have marched. That I have taken part in demonstrations. I have begged and pleaded. I have a history that has not been presented here. I have marched alongside black people for their rights. I have marched in support of jobs. I have a history of that. I have marched for access to decent housing. I have a history of that. I have marched against the war in Vietnam. I am a veteran of that war. And I have a history of that. What there is no history of is that your enemy tells you how you should act or how to carry out your struggle. Mr. Margolis intends to do precisely that. He stands there and has the gall to tell me how to wage my struggle. Mr. Margolis does not know how it feels to be a Puerto Rican in this country. Mr. Margolis does not know how it feels to be black in this country. He does not know the indignation one feels when the police, who supposedly represent law and order, call us "spic" or "nigger" and then spit in our face. I have had people spit in my face for being Puerto Rican. And I have been arrested for participating peacefully and legally in public demonstrations.

So that which Mr. Margolis alludes to does not exist. What does exist is a lie and a farce. And he is part of that lie and that farce. The United States Government is part of that lie and that farce. If I am standing here today, it is not because I lack the courage to fight, but rather because I have the courage to fight. I am certain, and will reaffirm, that Puerto Rico will be a free and sovereign nation.

I want to indicate to you that the evidence presented by the prosecutors will not show our great respect for human life, our appreciation of human life. The evidence will not tell you that Puerto Rico is a colony of the United States and that colonialism is a crime—and recognized as such by the international community.

---

[3] Court Record, 4–9.

The evidence will *not* show that Oscar López Rivera, the alleged terrorist, received military training in Cuba, nor in the Soviet Union. I received my military training at Fort Knox, Kentucky, and Fort Hood, Texas. I served in Vietnam. I served the imperialist government, the imperialist army of the United States. I was part of the United States military force in Vietnam. I served one year in Vietnam.

The evidence will not tell you that it was in Vietnam where I saw people fight against colonialism, where I saw people fight against imperialism. And where I learned how to develop such a struggle.

The evidence will not reveal anything about the colonial case of Puerto Rico. We will not hear anything about this subject. We will not hear anything regarding militarism in my country or how my country was conquered by force or how the popularly elected government was toppled and replaced by a military one.

We will see papers and documents depicting us as terrorists, but not see or hear anything about the United States policy of genocide toward my country. A policy which attempts to strip us of our language, our culture. A policy which has left sterile 40 percent of the women of reproductive age.

No one will tell you how and why half of our population, close to three million of my compatriots, were forced to immigrate to this country and live in the slums of New York and Chicago where they were subjected to social and institutional racism.

The government will introduce documents and make reference to Vieques Island. But they will not say anything about what is really going on in Vieques: the daily bombings, the destruction of the ecology, the killing and maiming of human beings caused by unexploded bombs, the destruction of the island's fishing industry and the control of the best land and fisheries by the United States Navy.

The government will present evidence showing some weapons. They are no more than a weapons collector would have at home. But the United States government will not show you the arsenal of weapons that the FBI uses in my country to terrorize and intimidate us. They will show you some sticks of dynamite which do not even amount to 150 pounds. But the United States government will not show you a bomb with a payload of 500 pounds, or that hundreds of such bombs are used daily in the U.S. Navy's bombing practice on the population of Vieques. . . .

The evidence will not tell you anything regarding the racist organizations created by the FBI and the CIA who have killed labor leaders and "independentistas." That they have bombed labor unions, student organizations, those of civic organizations such as the "Ateneo Puertorriqueño" and the Puerto Rico Bar Association.[4]

The United States government will not say that international organizations have determined that Puerto Rico is a colony of the United States and that, according to international law, they are committing a crime against my country. They will not tell you either that according to international law, when an anticolonial fighter is captured, as we were, he or she has the status of prisoner of war and should be judged by a competent international body.

I am addressing the people here, not because of the role you play, but rather in human terms. I am giving you the respect you deserve as human beings and I hope that what I have told you will make you think about the situation I have set forth, and that you can return to your communities and speak to them about the status of Puerto Rico, about the colonial pillaging of our nation, about the condition of oppression under which the people of Puerto Rico live. That is what this case is really about.

I want to close by saying that the United States government is using these illegal proceedings just as it did in 1936 and 1954 to see how it can put a stop to our fight in favor of freedom. Know by these precedents that history and justice are on our side.[5]

A Man in a Prison
Carlos Quiles
To Oscar López Rivera, prisoner of war, patriot

A man in a prison,
Another singing on a hill;

[4] The Puerto Rican Athenaeum, founded in 1876, is one of Puerto Rico's chief cultural institutions.

[5] Court Record, 4, 5, 30–44, 630–42.

The song becomes a dove
Of peace and liberation.

In the forge of Island fire
He melds all his passion
And livens his devotion
Of Patriot and *Borinqueño.*

Freedom is the dream
He holds in his heart
And urged by emotion
Of a *Boricua* song
Paints a window in his soul
A man in a prison.

The prisoner of war
Looks through this window
And from his spirit surges
Strong love for his land.
He feels his homeland encompass
All his faith and the aroma
Of freedom showing its face
To this window of the soul
Because sending him tranquility
Is another, singing on the hill.

Distance makes them closer
In a fleeting voyage of shooting stars
Because there is blood that is the trace
Of a national fragrance.

Then desires attacks
And tames them by the hand
The fire that makes them brothers;
The window to the soul opens,
The song becomes a dove.

Night to celebrate
In the jail of the tyrant
There the *Borincano* celebrates
With a warrior song

That song shall be heard
Day after day in prison
It is the song of a Nation
Of outrage imposed
And that song is a message
Of peace and liberation.

Three Kings Day, 2000

THE TORTURE OF IMPRISONMENT

★

> The memory of our pain deserves to be appreciated, remembered, and never denied.
> —Oscar López Rivera, March, 12, 1997

Oscar's voyage of terror through the gulag of the U.S. prison system began in 1981. The physical conditions, the abuse, and the torture of total isolation, sensory deprivation, and the degrading frequency of the naked full-body searches surpass Russian writer Alexander Solzhenitsyn's accounts about the Russian prisons of his time. Each of Oscar's transfers to the different prisons heightened the abuse and torture. Despite all the hard times and experiences imaginable, Oscar found the emotional support to face his jailers. His own words explain the source of some of his strength for resistance:

> Puerto Rican political prisoners and prisoners of war are the only ones who receive concrete support from a broad cross-section of their people. There are more New African political prisoners and their population is some fifteen times larger than ours in the diaspora, but if it weren't for sectors of white people, many of them would be rotting in the dungeon. There are many New Africans who have been languishing in prison for much longer than we have, but the vast majority of their people don't even know that they are in jail, much less why. The same can be said about the North American political prisoners. i have done time with Native American, New African, and white political prisoners and prisoners of war. In the case of one of the Native Americans, his support base came from the whites and from the international community, but the support was scant from his own people.
>
> And the situation of the North Americans was about the same. . . .This has not been the case for us. Whether a lot or a little, we have always received support. Even in the demonstrations here in the Marion gulag, the Puerto Rican presence has been predominant (Evaluation, 1990).

Four North American prisons have swallowed thirty years of Oscar's life. The first was in Leavenworth, Kansas. His confinement there extended from 1981 to 1986.

Upon arrival at the institution, the majority of the prison guards were waiting for him. They surrounded him and verbally assaulted him. They repeatedly stressed that they didn't want him there; that he was a dangerous terrorist and the place for him was Marion: an even higher-security prison, regarded among prison guards as the right place to eliminate terrorists. Marion was consistent with what the FBI and the U.S. Department of Justice established as public policy with respect to Puerto Rico: "The potential terrorist elements are the *independentistas*; only one side can survive.

If the terrorist cannot be neutralized, death is the only way to stop him from repeating his actions. A terrorist cannot be rehabilitated."[1]

This policy is the one that guided the new super-maximum-security prison in Marion: finding the ways to drive the prisoner insane or get him to commit suicide.

Oscar managed to evade the provocations. In 1985, his jailers reported, "In this institution he was assigned to the paint shop and to the institutional laundry room receiving average and above-average evaluations at work. He demonstrated favorable adjustment and maintained positive relations with the staff, and he participated in some of the programmed educational activities."[2] He took advantage of the opportunities for higher education and completed 104 hours of accredited studies by the University of Kansas and a community college.

Despite his positive conduct, the personal harassment by his jailers never ceased. Oscar described in a letter home one particularly repugnant example of the prison system's abuse of medical procedures to intimidate and persecute him:

> Because my father had died of colon cancer, i had requested a test when i reached age 40. The doctor told me he was going to send me to the VA Hospital to have a lower GI performed. He believed it was the fastest way to have it done. One morning, as i was coming out of the mess hall, after eating breakfast, two guards approached me and told me i was going for a trip. They took me to R&D (Receiving and Discharge), stripped and searched me, and gave me a set of clothes, placed me in leg irons and black box, and took me out to the VA Hospital.[3] They took me to an area where a

[1] Luis Nieves Falcón, *Un Siglo de Represión Política en Puerto Rico, 1898–1998* (San Juan: The Institute of Caribbean Studies/Instituto de Estudios Caribeños, 2009), 81.

[2] USP Leavenworth prison records, June 18, 1986.

[3] The black box goes over the middle of the handcuffs and has a hole for a lock. The chain that goes around the waist is fastened around the black box and locked on the side, controlling the prisoner's hand movements.

man was waiting. He told me i was going to be given a lower GI. i told him i had just had breakfast and that i knew i had to be prepared from the day before if i were going to have such an examination. He told me to try anyway. i was given a barium enema and told to do it by myself. After i did it i was taken to the radiology department. When i told the radiologist i had had breakfast, he said he couldn't give me the test. When i returned to the prison i went to the doctor and told him about what had happened. Two weeks later i was called to the hospital. When i arrived at the hospital i was told to get my hygiene gear and i did, returned to the hospital, and i was locked in a cell. It was on a Thursday. Friday no one came for me. Later in the day i was given a meal. On Saturday i saw the head doctor walking past the cell and i started banging on the door and calling him. He was surprised to see there was someone in the cell. i told him i had been placed there on Thursday and had not been seen by any medical staff. i reminded him i was not an animal and that he wasn't a veterinarian. He told me he knew nothing about my situation, but that he was going to find out. About half an hour later he came and told me i wasn't a medical case but rather a security one. i asked him if he could allow me to make a legal phone call and he allowed me to do it. i called Atty. Melinda Power at Westtown Law Office. Four days later i was awakened at 2:00 a.m. and asked to strip while two lieutenants (Graham and Smith (AKA "Shitty Smithy")) watched me get dressed. They refused to allow me to put on my glasses and my watch. (The watch was a gift from sister Clary.) They escorted me to the rear gate and made me stand between the two gates for over an hour. i was wearing a short sleeved shirt and a pair of Peter Pan shoes and the temperature was 27°. An hour later, about five vehicles showed up. They threw me in the back seat of one and at high speed i was taken to the airport in Ft. Leavenworth. From there i was flown to Springfield. i was kept in Springfield for 22 days and returned to Leavenworth. When i was given my property, my watch and glasses were missing.

Such abuse can only be understood in the context of the government's ongoing attack on Oscar, whose daily movements were under surveillance to create a negative record of his conduct. The FBI sent informants who were placed in his unit. Their mission was to get close to him, to ask trick questions, and produce prejudicial witnesses. Their specific assignment was to fabricate an escape conspiracy in order to make a case against him.

The entrapment plan was eventually successful, and on June 18, 1986, they accused him of planning an escape using a helicopter, explosives, and firearms. He was immediately given a disciplinary transfer to the Marion Penitentiary on June 24, 1986. Charges were filed against him in the U.S. District Court for the Northern District of Illinois. The court proceedings lasted from September 1986 until February 1988. During this period, he was transferred to MCC, Chicago. Here they kept him in total segregation. He could not be out of the cell with other inmates and had a four-man order placed on him; a lieutenant and four guards had to be available to take him out of the cell. The institutional facilities accessible to other inmates were denied to him. In fact, he couldn't use the minimal law library available in the prison. He was allowed to receive only hour-long visits. A very small space served for legal and social visits. The cell did not have adequate heating and in the winter it was like a refrigerator, unbearable.

During the trial, he affirmed the lack of jurisdiction of the Court and revealed the transformation of the term "Puerto Rican" into a linguistic term used at the service of his aggressors. His confrontation with said court went as follows:

> Good morning, members of the jury. My presence in this room, the fact that I am addressing you, and any other intervention that I might make in these proceedings, should not be misconstrued as a defense on my behalf. I appear before you, not to defend myself, but with the hope of sharing with you some ideas, some experiences, some facts that can help you, members of the jury, to have a clearer appreciation of this case.
>
> On several occasions I have informed the Court, Judge Hart, that I do not recognize the ju-

risdiction of the United States government over me, nor the jurisdiction of this Court to judge me and criminalize me . . .

This position I have taken is rooted in an indelible, historical fact; a fact beyond my power to control. That fact is that I was born 44 years ago in the colony of Puerto Rico. . . . As a colonized person, from the day of my birth to the moment of my death, I bear the chains and shackles of colonialism, regardless of whether I am in Puerto Rico, here, or any other place in the world. I would like to share an experience with you that will show you precisely what it is that I am talking about.

Colonialism, dear members of the jury, is a monumental injustice according to the norms of civilized humanity and a crime under international law. According to United Nations Resolution 2621, the continuation of colonialism in all its forms and manifestations is a crime that constitutes a violation of the charter of the United Nations, Resolution 1514 (XV), the Declaration on the Granting of Independence to Colonial Countries and Peoples. . . . No nation, ladies and gentlemen, has the right to take over another nation. . . . No nation has the right to nullify the sovereignty of another nation. The military invasion and occupation of Puerto Rico clearly depicts the rapacious and voracious nature of the United States government, with the armed forces, rifles, and cannons it used to subjugate a people into submission and reduce a nation of one million inhabitants to a commodity for the bartering of human beings.

For 89 years, this nation, conquered by force—the Puerto Rican people—have been denied their basic rights to self-determination and independence. This may seem a great irony to all of us, because the perpetrator of this injustice is a nation that claims to be the world leader of freedom and democracy: the United States of America. . . . But the sad truth is that to this day . . . the rifle, cannon, and prison cell are still used to subjugate those of us who want a free nation.

During slavery, the government had two categories: the good slave and the bad slave. The good slave was the one who was submissive, who followed the orders of the master, who, at the order of the master was willing to inflict whatever harm on his fellow slaves. . . . In contrast, the bad slave was the one who sought his freedom. He was bad if he wanted to liberate his people . . . he was bad if he wanted to put an end to the degrading and pernicious system of slavery.

In the case of Puerto Rico we can say that there are also two categories that are applicable: the good Puerto Rican is the one who is willing to tolerate the indignity and tyranny of colonialism. The good Puerto Rican is the one willing to support the interests of the United States in Puerto Rico. The good Puerto Rican is the one who is willing to be cannon fodder in the wars waged by the United States. . . . The bad Puerto Rican, on the other hand, is the one who wants his freedom, who wants the freedom of his nation and the freedom of his people. Therefore, he is bad.

I can tell you I have been both: I have been a good Puerto Rican and a bad Puerto Rican.

I was a good Puerto Rican in 1965. I was drafted and served in the United States Army. I went to Vietnam. I fought in Vietnam. I served a year in Vietnam. I was good enough to be awarded a Bronze Star by the Secretary of the Army for meritorious service, valor, and courage under hostile fire. I was a good Puerto Rican because I went to Vietnam to fight against people who had done nothing to me and I went there to fight against them. I carried an M-16 rifle and grenades. I shot at Vietnamese people. They shot at me. For that I was a good Puerto Rican.

When I came back to this country, as soon as I expressed my opposition to the war in Vietnam, as a veteran, not as someone who had gone to Canada or Europe, but as someone who had served, I became a bad Puerto Rican. I became a bad Puerto Rican when I tried to struggle to improve the living conditions

> of my people. I firmly believe in justice and that those who are dispossessed of their essential rights should have some power, at least the opportunity to recover the rights to be full citizens . . . I marched and I struggled for better housing for the marginalized in the city of Chicago, for jobs, for a better education, for alternative schools. But more than anything, I struggled to help the Puerto Rican people—my own people.
>
> Despite all these struggles, as a Puerto Rican, I have to seek the independence of my homeland. I can do no other.[4]

He was sentenced on February 26, 1988, to a fifteen-year term, consecutive to his prior fifty-five year sentence, increasing his sentence to seventy years. He was imprisoned at Marion from 1988 to 1994.

The purpose of the Marion prison is to destroy the individual assigned to serve his sentence there. Sensory deprivation, extended isolation, and strip searches are common. The ultimate goal: to make the prisoner to go insane or commit suicide.

What was the written opinion of the jailers about Oscar López Rivera?

> His initial adjustment was favorable. He was assigned tasks as a barber and as an orderly in the general population units and has constantly received above-average to excellent evaluations. He has kept a clear conduct/ a low profile and he shows a mature and cordial attitude in his interactions with staff and the unit team. He is not considered to be a person with serious management problems. Due to his continuing display of appropriate institutional adjustment he has been considered for transfer to another unit, but on four occasions said transfer has been denied due to his refusal to work

[4] Court Record, 455–77.

> in UNICOR.[5] He is classified as a high/maximum security inmate.[6]

What were the jail conditions imposed on a person with the positive behavior that the jailers themselves describe? Oscar himself described it as follows:

> Alexander Solzhenitsyn coined the word "Gulag" to describe the oppressive, abusive and destructive regimen that defined the daily life of a political prisoner or a prisoner of conscience in the Soviet Union. i use the word "spiritcide" to describe the dehumanizing and pernicious existence that i have suffered since i have been a prisoner, particularly the years that i have been in this dungeon (labyrinth). It is spiritcide because the death and annihilation of the spirit are what the jailers are seeking by keeping me in such deleterious conditions. i face, on the one hand, an environment that is a sensory deprivation laboratory, and on the other hand, a regimen replete with obstacles to deny, destroy or paralyze my creativity. We know that sensory deprivation and the denial of creative activity causes the spirit to wither and die. That is exactly what the jailers are seeking by keeping me here.
>
> i am locked up in a cell that is 6' wide and 9' long, for an average of 22 1/2 hours a day. Today, as i write this letter, i have spent 36 hours without going out and if they don't take us out tomorrow, three days will have passed without moving from the same space. i have to do everything in this tiny space—from eating my meals to going to the bathroom. So it is dining room and toilet at the same time. My bed is a cement slab.

---

[5] UNICOR, or Federal Prison Industries, is a U.S. government-owned corporation, which solicits prisoners to work in production of goods which are then sold for profit. Criticized for providing often unsafe working conditions and "slave wages" even in the context of prison pay (sometimes as low as 23 cents per hour), UNICOR is supposed to be a voluntary program, giving inmates the choice to work outside of regularly required prison-based jobs.

[6] Official Report of USP Marion.

And the whole cell is monochromatic—painted a dead yellow. From an aesthetic point of view, it is as attractive an animal's cage in the zoo.

Living in these conditions day after day and year after year has to have an adverse effect on my senses. i don't have access to fresh air or to natural light because even when i turn off the light in the cell to sleep, the guards keep the outside lights on and light enters the cell. All i can say is that i only see the shadow of the shadow, but not the object. i have lived like that for five years, without seeing a starry sky or the darkness of night.

Day and night i hear the roaring of the electric fans, whose noise is so strident that when i don't hear them, i feel disoriented. When i go to the visiting room it takes me a while to reorient my ears. When they take me out to the yard, once a week for two hours, the singing of the birds is like music to my ears. It's as if they woke up and were freed from their confinement. That is when i have the opportunity to appreciate the difference and realize the detrimental effect of the conditions and the noise that prevail here.

i think that while sensory deprivation is very harmful, the denial of creativity is even more so. Without the opportunity to be creative, the individual cannot self-realize. And without self-realization, people become alienated and go to waste. If people do not reach their creative potential through self-realization, they can be reduced to domestic animals, or to the existence of a caged animal in the zoo.

The 22 1/2 hours that i am inside the cell every day is time that i could use to be more creative and at least make a small contribution to my people. But in order to punish me, the jailers deny me every opportunity to use my time doing creative endeavors. For example, a year ago i started to experiment with acrylic paints. i practiced with the paints every day for a couple of hours. i felt useful and whiled the time with them. But for the jailers my experiment with the paints was an impediment that neutralized their punishment. So, they decided to declare the acrylic paints a threat to prison security and confiscated them. Such nonsense could only be thought up by goons with twisted and perverse minds. Unfortunately, that is their mentality. They get their jollies by making life as miserable as possible for the prisoner. And since our hands are tied, they do what they want with us.

It is not that i don't know how or can't keep myself occupied. i read and write every day. i also do my exercises to take care of my health. But after reading 3 or 4 newspapers, 5 or more magazines, and a novel or two, or a book, the routine gets monotonous. The same thing happens with writing. In addition, reading and writing here are uncomfortable. The writing routine gets even harder because with every day that passes, i feel more disconnected and distanced from the people who are my audience. After 10 years of being in jail i can't even get in touch and communion with my family and other beloved ones. This lack of communion and communication affects my writing. With every day that goes by, the gap grows wider and writing becomes more difficult.

Now that so many years have gone by, i have to ask myself if what i'm doing in this dungeon isn't an exercise in futility. If i read something interesting, if i learn something new, who do i share it with? Over the course of time in prison, i have learned that communication from here is a word without wings. If i write them sometimes they remain lifeless on the paper and if i speak them they don't move beyond the immediate space.

So, it shouldn't be a surprise to anyone why i feel that what i read and write amount to a futile exercise. And since i detest futility, sometimes i lose the desire to fulfill these tasks.

There are other factors that feed that sense of futility. The total and absolute censorship practiced by the jailers affects my desire to express myself. There is no way for me to express myself freely without the fear of giving the enemy the chance to know me better. i cannot provide my enemy information about my state of mind. And each time i write about the situation here and how it's affecting me, i am giving my enemy information that can be used against me.

i am never sure where my writings will end up, nor when the enemy will confiscate what i have written. In 1986 i lost all the material that i had been writing for over 5 years. i was never able to get it back. After losing what you have written, you cannot replicate it. So it was a total loss. Last year once again i lost my written matter. The loss of material through confiscation, censorship, and distance from my audience are factors that inhibit me and sap my desire to write. i feel like someone who lives with a broken roof, so that when it rains, i am deluged.

The cumulative effect of all these experiences, added to the punishment of being in prison under such deleterious conditions and in such a depressing environment, is wearing down my spirit little by little. i constantly have to search for the energy to renew my determination and vitality. i cannot, for one instant, lose sight of the sinister and ubiquitous gaze of the executioners who, like predators, are just looking for the right moment to kill my spirit.

i am aware that there are people who say that we have to take the consequences. Perhaps there are others who say that we are getting the punishment we deserve. Without judging the people who think that way, i say that no one who is just, who is sensitive, who respects the inalienable rights of humanity, and who loves the truth could justify the existence of a gulag like the one i am in. In our case, imprisoned as we are for loving and defending our homeland, the United States government has no reason to punish us under such pernicious conditions.

i do not want to give anyone the impression that this is the end of everything. We know that human beings have the capacity to adapt to everything. If there were prisoners who adapted and survived in the concentration camps in Hitler's Germany, we too can adapt and survive. The question is, at what price?

Just like the German concentration camps where the guards became beasts and committed the worse brutalities, the same things happen here. The guards are not exempt from becoming beasts. They have the capacity to commit the worst crimes and the meanest acts. The dehumanization we suffer as prisoners at the hands of the jailers also affects the guards, dehumanizing them and transforming them into beasts. How long can such an abominable reality be justified and accepted?

i know that the human spirit has the capacity to resurrect after suffering spiritcide. And like the rose or the wilted leaf falls and dies and in its place a newer and stronger one is reborn or resurrects, my spirit will also resurrect if the jailers achieve their goals.

What gives me the certainty that my spirit will be reborn after this difficult test is not an enigma that must be deciphered. My certainty lies in my confidence that i have chosen to serve a just and noble cause. A free, just, and democratic homeland represents a sublime ideal worth fighting for. There is an organic relationship between my motivation to struggle and that ideal.

i know material poverty as i know my own hands. i know the pain caused by material poverty and spiritual poverty. i know the pain of stubbing a toe on a stump for lack of shoes to wear. i know the pain of hunger. Because i have suffered in flesh, bone, and spirit, i reject and i detest material poverty as much as spiritual poverty. And maybe i detest the latter more than the former because it is causes more ignorance and insensitivity.

Spiritual poverty nurtures ignorance and robs us of our conscience. And if we are ignorant and lack consciousness, we exist without a human purpose. i am a witness to how harmful ignorance and lack of consciousness are. Let us see: the first time that i identified with the Puerto Rican flag was in Vietnam. A Boricua fellow soldier had one painted on the camouflage of his helmet. It caught my attention and i also painted one. Afterward i saw other Boricuas who had done the same thing and it became a symbol of Puerto Rican identity. i was over 22 years old when i discovered the Puerto

Rican flag. What is incongruent and disconcerting about this experience are the age, place, and circumstances where it took place. A Puerto Rican, colonized down to the marrow, fighting a war created to protect and defend the hegemony of the economic interests of his colonizer, discovers his flag, having done nothing to defend it.

i had lived in Puerto Rico for the first 14 years of my life and had gone to school there up through the middle of ninth grade, but i had never identified with the Puerto Rican flag. In fact, i don't remember ever having seen the Puerto Rican flag waving in the schools where i studied. i knew the United States flag well and unconsciously defended it. This is because i was ignorant and had no consciousness of the Puerto Rican colonial reality. i was even ready to give my life for the nation and the government system responsible for the debacle suffered by my native country. So for me, the eradication of ignorance and becoming conscious are part of my struggle against spiritual and material poverty.

i am in this dungeon and the possibility that i will be freed is remote, not to say impossible, under conditions equal to or worse than caged animals, under spiritual and physical attack, but with full dignity and with a clean and clear conscience. i speak of this painful test not to provoke pity or lament but to offer to those who may be interested my interpretation of my existence in this gulag. i use the word "interpretation" because it is a subjective narrative and subjectivity is not always identical to the facts. i have no desire to color appearances and pass them off as facts of the absolute truth. i am interested in the hearts and minds of those who love justice and seek the truth. i am not interested in vulgar sentimentality. And even though the silence of the outside is more painful than the solitude inside the hole, a bird's song or the sound of a cicada always reaches my ears to awaken my faith and keep me keeping on.

At one time, i thought that if i struggled with great dedication and commitment, i could perhaps bequeath my daughter and her generation a free Puerto Rico,

> with a democratic and just government. My daughter is a mother. Now that i am a grandfather i have to ask myself what future awaits my granddaughter Karina. i only hope that she and her generation have the consciousness and spiritual strength to be outraged and continue the struggle if our homeland is still being trampled upon. i know that if we dare to struggle, triumph is imminent, and that for those who struggle, victory is their reward.

The jailers did not let up in their persecution. Solitary confinement did not satisfy them. And, faced with the possibility of a transfer to another institution, they intensified the hate campaign against Oscar. On March 30, 1990, after having been ordered to come out of his cell for an inspection—something unusual, since inspections are usually done in front of the inmate—he was accused of having a sharp object to open locks found in his cell. On June 30, 1990, he was removed from the transfer list and sentenced to ninety days of absolute segregation in what is known as "the hole."

The retaliation against a person whose spirit they cannot break, whose resistance is greater than their oppression, did not cease. The acrylic paints he used for painting were declared a threat to prison security and the creative activity was abruptly interrupted. In spite of these retaliatory moves and the fact that he could no longer paint with acrylics, he was able to face the challenge and looked for alternatives in order to continue playing with colors. Some images of his work appear here.

The continuous chain of injustices did not overcome him. The ongoing correspondence with his family sustained him. He told his sister Mercedes, "In most cases, when you need something, you approach the family. i hope that ours continues to practice unity. Even if it is from a distance, all the moments you celebrate together, i will enjoy vicariously." In the same letter, he sent his family advice about his daughter and granddaughter.

On September 20, 1994, he gave his opinion about social changes in Puerto Rico: "The dispersion of the family and the atomization of the community have provoked damaging changes, including the practice of lending a hand to a neighbor or to your 'compadre' or 'comadre' when needed. . . . Take good care of yourself and pa'lante always."

Despite everything, Oscar always sends greetings for the end of the year, as he did on December 13, 1994: "i hope you decide to celebrate Christmas. Even if for a little while, take the time and enjoy it. Best wishes to you and to all! With much love!!"

LIFE IS A CONSTANT STRUGGLE

★

> It is much easier not to struggle, to give up and take the path of the living dead. But if we want to live, we must struggle.
> —Oscar López Rivera, 1991

With increasing spotlights on the illegal and repressive conditions in the U.S. Penitentiary at Marion, it soon became the Achilles' heel of the U.S. prison system. Criticisms voiced in the United States were joined by some of the best known international human rights organizations across the globe.[1] The eventual elimina-

[1] In 2006, after years of protest, Marion was "downgraded" to a medium-security prison, with major renovations made, including the elimination of the "control unit" subprisons. The renovations enabled Marion to increase its incarcerated population from below four hundred to over nine hundred inmates.

tion of the best-known U.S. torture center did not bring about an end to torture. On the contrary, a new determination was born to create a maximum-security superprison.

On December 21, 1994, Oscar was transferred to the new prison, widely considered to supplant Marion's title as the worst prison in the country in its treatment toward inmates. It violated (and violates) most of the internationally accepted standards for the treatment of inmates. In Florence, Colorado, Oscar began his writings about his experiences there by explaining that it was supported by the local community. Oscar believed that to be true because, as he stated on December 30, 1994:

> At a cost of more than $200 million in construction expenses, the Florence gulag generates more than $60 million per year. This money ends up in banks, stores, real estate businesses, car dealers, fast food chains, and even the politicians from Florence and the surrounding communities. Therefore, for the Florence community the gulags represent a gold mine that will supply money indefinitely. It doesn't matter that the town of Florence lives off the suffering and misery of the prisoners that are warehoused in the gulags. The first reason for the change of attitude and the prison building frenzy is the large amount of money they generate.

Further, that same month, he provided us a detailed description to enable us to understand the irrational reality and structured dehumanization that prevails in the Florence gulag:

> i would like to start by describing what seems to me is the most noticeable physical trait of the gulag. It is a concrete and steel labyrinth, painted almost completely white, built to isolate and disable the prisoner. Each unit is isolated from the others, each cell block is isolated from the others, and each cell is isolated from the others. The inmate can see nothing of the outside except for a small piece of sky from the cell's window (4 1/4 inches wide, 4 feet long).

The construction model resembles that of the notorious Pelican Bay State Prison in California. Every unit has an electronic control center from which all cell doors, cell blocks, offices, and recreation areas are remotely controlled. Nothing moves unless monitored from the electronic control equipment's sheltered booth.

Each cell is divided in two parts. The entrance is a solid steel door. There is a sally port between the steel door and the second door. The second entrance is barred. To remove the inmate from the cell, the prison guards (always at least four) ask Control to open the solid door. Two come in. The inmate puts his hands through a hole in the barred door. The guard cuffs him and never releases him. They order Control to open the second door and the inmate walks backward into the hallway, controlled by the officer all the time. The inmate is shaken down immediately and frisked from head to toe with a metal detector.

The cell has adequate natural and electric lighting. Everything is built in concrete—bed, desk, shelf, and the stool to sit on. It has a toilet, sink, shower, cold and hot water. The only thing it lacks is fresh air. The heating system is central and the cell is hermetically sealed.

i have two problems with the cell's lack of fresh air. My skin dries up. The first eight days after arriving, my skin was flaking up in scales. Because i was exposed to Agent Orange in Vietnam, i have skin problems. My other problem is that every time i sneeze, my nose bleeds. i use oil for my dry skin, and it helps.

Exercise and Recreation: There are two types of recreation areas here. What they call the "outside rec" area is like a concrete yard, with a basketball hoop and an area to play handball. It has a pull-up and dips stand, a toilet, and drinking water. It is surrounded by a concrete wall, which is sheltered by huge steel beams covered with cyclone fence wire. All cell windows face the yard. The light and sky we see is what filters through the yard's roof. The ground is built unevenly, so there is no point where you can stand evenly. Since i run, one side of the body is always higher than the other.

> The indoor recreation area consists of two rooms: each a little larger than a cell. It has a pull-up and dips stand. They are tightly closed. They don't have water or a toilet. They're so hot and filthy that almost nobody uses them. After going there twice, i now refuse to go again.
>
> The average time for outside recreation and exercise is 10 to 12 hours a week. We go out for two hours at a time. If the weather is cold or if it's snowing, we are not taken outside.
>
> All visits are through a telephone. The inmate sits on a concrete stool in a tightly closed room. The visitor is on the other side of the glass. There is room for only one visitor. The inmate can only see his visitor, he cannot see if there are other inmates in the visiting area. i haven't seen any vending machines in the visitors' area. There is a camera in the inmates' little room, and in the visitors' area there are also cameras. Everything is being watched and recorded. My first visit, i went through two strip-searches before the visit and two after, despite having been chained and watched by five officers all the time from the cell to the visiting room. For a visit with my lawyer i was put through one strip-search before and one after, and was cuffed with my hands behind my back. For my family's visit, i was shackled and they put on the black box.

His granddaughter Karina, daughter of Clarissa and the son of Puerto Rican former political prisoner Carmen Valentin, offers her opinion about the visits to Marion and then Florence:

> My first visits to my grandfather were in the federal prison in Marion, Illinois.
>
> They only allowed in two adults and three minors. My mom tells me that they only let her bring in three diapers and 12 ounces of milk. Marion was a Control Unit and we could only see grandpa Oscar—we couldn't touch him and he could not touch us. We were separated by glass. For many years, putting my hands against the glass was my way of playing with my grandfather. There was no

The family in San Sebastián,
Puerto Rico

Oscar as a young man: a decorated veteran

Growing up: in
the 1960s and '70s

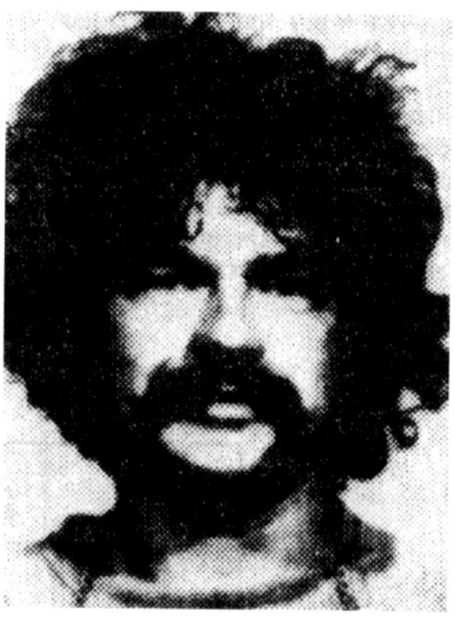

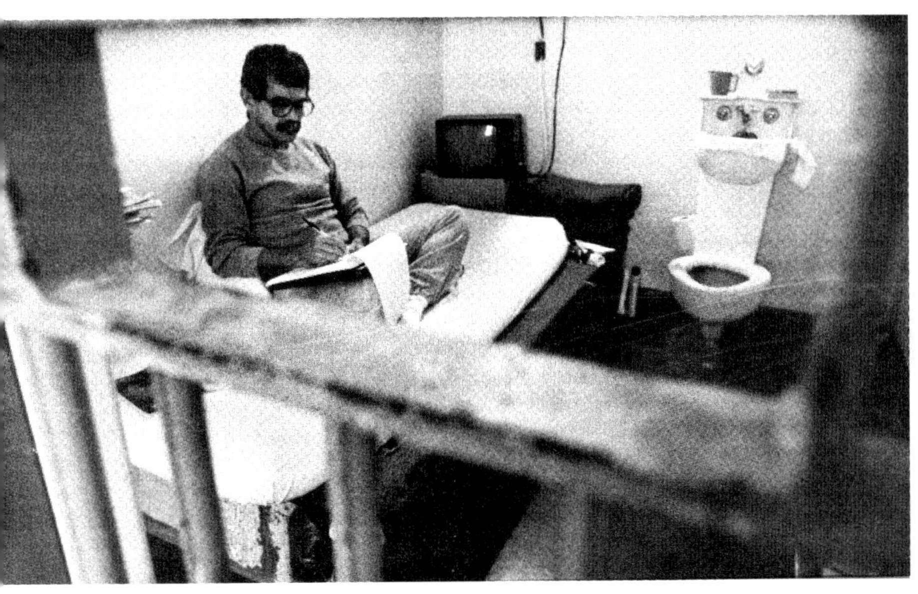

Not enough space: Oscar in his cell

With sister Clary López

Prison visits with family

With daughter Clarissa and the next generation

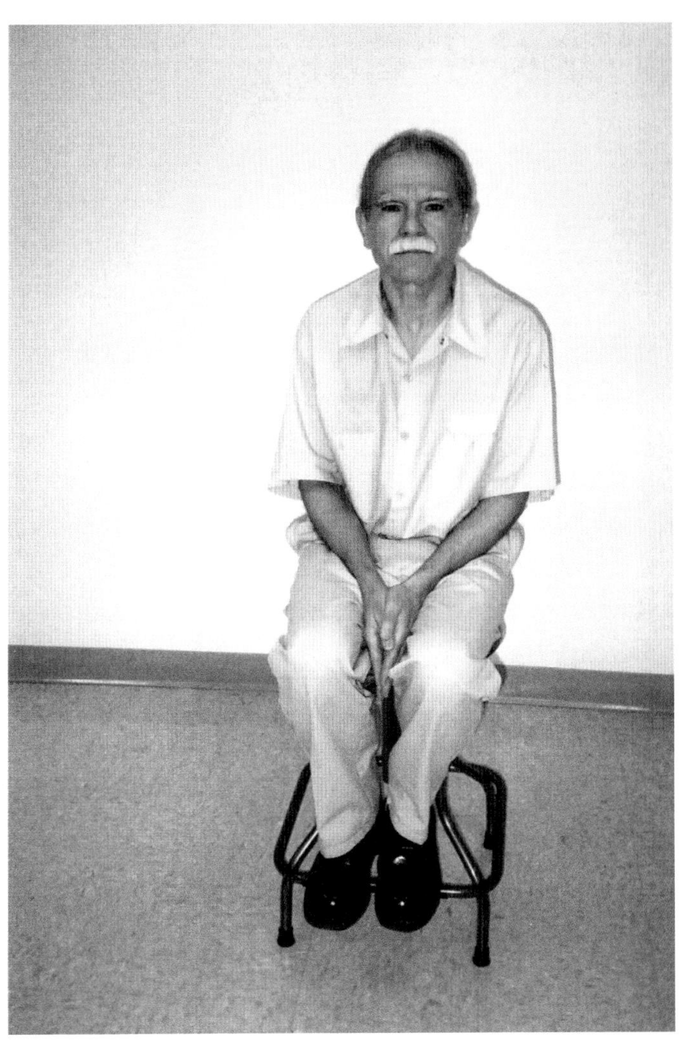

Some recent portraits by Oscar

OLR

Banner drops for Oscar

yard or swings at Marion, and the guards were hostile. Grandpa Oscar was escorted by 4 or 5 guards. He was the only prisoner they always brought in like that.

Later, Grandpa Oscar was transferred to the prison in Florence, Colorado. The visiting room there was underground.

You went through three checkpoints on the way in and on the way you could tell we were going to the basement. The room was painted beige and grandpa's clothes were the same color. I don't have photos of me and grandpa in Marion or Florence because photographs were not allowed.

Oscar continues his report in February 1995:

The educational and library services are very limited. The inmate is given a list of library books. So far i haven't seen any book that would spark my interest. The selection of books in Spanish is very limited and they are almost all from non-Latin authors. The Director of the Education Department has told me that they are still trying to organize the programs. They will offer elementary school classes and General Equivalency Diploma courses.

The Department of Recreation offers passive games, like Bingo. i don't participate in such activities. The director told me that they still haven't organized the program for the inmates who do artwork.

According to the Hospital Director, professional medical services will be contracted from doctors in the area. i believe that the doctor is brought to the unit, just as the barber is brought to give the inmates their haircuts. i still don't know anyone who has requested dental services. From what i have seen on paper, the inmate is offered the same services as in Marion. Since i don't request medical services, i cannot give an exact account.

There are two chaplains that frequently visit each cell. Both are very polite. i only exchange greetings with them. They always ask if everything is okay. They offer religious services through a TV network. Thus far, i have seen that they respond well to inmates' requests.

i still haven't seen a legal library, so i can't say anything, except that there is one. An inmate told me he used it.

Each cell has a television set with four radio stations. The prison guards use the TV set to communicate to the inmates any information and programs. There is no access to public radio or TV stations.

We are allowed two phone calls a month, fifteen minutes each. The inmate has to pay for the calls. The phone can be used every day, from 6:00 p.m. to 9:00 p.m. The prison guards bring the phone to the cell and we dial through the bars. It can be used without much trouble. All conversations are monitored.

i had a legal phone call with a lawyer. Even though the distance from the cell to the office where i received the call is less than 30 meters, i was shackled and cuffed with the black box and submitted to a strip-search before and after the call. Two officers watched me while i spoke with the lawyer. There is no way of knowing if the call is being monitored.

Up until now, everything indicates that the prison guards want to discourage social/family and legal visits, and legal phone calls. They make everything complicated and difficult.

We use the same attire as other high security prisons. The only difference is that each time the inmates are taken outside the unit, they must wear a white jumpsuit. i have a personal wardrobe for exercising—sweaters, running shoes, and tennis shorts.

i have never used the grievance system, so i don't know how the jailers respond to complaints. All my conversations regarding any problems have been with the unit manager, who is of Mexican descent.

Access to written material, like newspapers, magazines, and books, is much more limited here than in Marion. There, inmates shared written material. Here, the inmate cannot share anything, which gives us very limited access to news and information. The fact that we only have access to four radio stations and four private T.V. stations also reduces our access to news and information.

Yesterday, an inmate received his first visit through the Prisoner's Visitation Project. So they are allowing at least that organization's visits. i believe it will be the only organization that will be allowed to visit the inmates.

The biggest problem an inmate faces here is sleep deprivation. i'm woken up every hour each night. The night count starts at 10:00 p.m. and takes place every half hour. i still haven't been able to sleep for a period of more than 50 minutes without interruption. Experts say that humans need to sleep for a period of more than three hours without interruption in order to achieve a restful state. Since i can barely sleep well through the night, i wake up feeling haggard.

There are only four inmates in my cell block, but one of them has a long history of mental problems and has been under behavior modification drugs. He spends all day and night screaming obscenities and fighting his war against invisible enemies. Why is this inmate here? Sometimes he starts to scream at three in the morning. i can't sleep with all the noise.

At the beginning, i said that this gulag is a steel and concrete labyrinth built to isolate and disable. Here, the inmate has no contact with other inmates outside of the exercise and recreation periods. The goal is to isolate the prisoner so that no solidarity is developed. Cells are built to guarantee such isolation. At night a hole in the solid door is opened so that the inmates can yell to each other. But such yelling is not a synonym of conversation and dialogue; what it does is disturb and upset those who don't take part. i have said that what they want here is to make us as mute as the walls and steel bars. The inmate is also intimidated into keeping quiet because here even the doors have ears. And the guards let the inmates know about this. So the idea of a private conversation with another inmate is unthinkable.

Prisoners need solidarity and help. There are inmates that don't receive any letters. In a place like Marion, i could give stamps or coffee to another inmate. i could share reading material. Those who had nothing always found help.

In Marion, i went to the yard once a week, and from there i saw trees, animals, birds . . . i heard the noise of the train, and the singing of the cicadas. i ran on the soil and could smell it. i could be surrounded by butterflies and could touch the grass with my hands. But there is none of that here.

Dialogue is something that was practiced in Marion. i could always find another inmate who was interested in political issues. If an inmate needed help in terms of schooling, one could give it to him. If an inmate wanted to learn something, there was always someone who could teach him. But what will happen here to the inmates who don't have anything? What will happen to those who need psychological help? Without solidarity or any type of support, those who have nothing will be the most vulnerable. That is cruel.

We are talking about depriving and denying the prisoner of very human and necessary things—use of oral language and words, solidarity and support, sleep and rest, tranquility, and, above all, access to nature. And what perhaps is most deleterious and abominable is the type of relationship that exists between the prison guards and the inmates. The prison guards are mentally programmed to execute the program and the mission of this gulag. The vision and the program justify the stigmatizing and dehumanization of prisoners. Prisoners who are sent here are considered beasts, predators, and animals. They are stereotyped and stigmatized without any impartial judgment and evaluation. Since the guards are mentally programmed and their minds are full of ill will and stupidity, they can justify anything, even the most flagrant and gross abuse because, for them, the inmate deserves it.

But the guards are not alone, and they don't act without orders from higher up. They receive their mandate from the outside community. Their neighbors, the town of Florence—which violated its conscience by agreeing to live off the suffering and pain of the prisoners—give the jailers their orders. And they were the first who justified the gulag's construction in this area. And even above the town's authority, are the bureaucrats and social engineers of the Bureau of Prisons, political hacks, and the prison industry. Nowadays, the prison industry is one of the strongest and biggest growing in Gringoland. And it is this industry which mobilizes its resources to build more and more prisons, each time even more severe and more dehumanizing.

Finally, i would like you to know how i arrived here. The jailers at Marion refused to give me a transfer because, when i arrived there in 1986, i informed them that i would not work in their UNICOR because it produced material for the United States Armed Forces, which constituted a violation of my political principles. The jailers always had a perfect excuse to keep me at Marion.

Kathleen Hawk, Director of the Federal Bureau of Prisons, testified before a subcommittee from Congress on May 19, 1994 that her agency's policy stated that prisoners could not be forced to work for UNICOR. But, in spite of this, they tried to force me and other prisoners. If, according to its director, the Bureau's policy states that inmates cannot be forced to work in the factories, then why was i forced? Who is following policies, the prison guards or me? By refusing to go against my conscience, i become a predator and a demon?

It is common knowledge that the reasons to justify building this dungeon are apocryphal accounts, for there are no facts to back them up. It is also known that its construction is based on a policy of hate and fear. This makes it an irrational policy and, therefore, to legitimize itself it has to stigmatize and dehumanize the inmate. If we take all this into account, you can understand why we are here.

The family correspondence between Oscar and his sister, Mercedes, reveals once again the primary relationship which exists among his relatives in spite of the distance between them.

Through letters, he still performed his role as counselor in controversial situations that developed in the family; he also accurately analyzed Puerto Rico's situation, and frankly critiqued the work being done toward his liberation. He also frankly described his situation in captivity to his loved ones, and did not miss any opportunity to offer orientation referring to his artwork.

Regarding his family, his major worry was his mother Mita's battle with Alzheimer's disease. He reported on February 20, 1995:

> During these past years, the illness has received a lot of publicity. . . . i have been able to see very informative programs. . . . One recommendation they make is that the person should keep busy. They say that people with Alzheimer's can be stimulated through music because they can perceive sounds very well. This helps control erratic behavior. . . . i think that if Mita can be kept entertained, it can help prevent behavior from being too erratic. . . . No one should be kept in the dark about her illness and how she is responding. It helps a lot to have everything out in the open

In conclusion, he expressed on April 16, 1995, his belief that "Mita's case, as well as those of other people who suffer from this disease, can be used to educate the public. . . . So it's up to all of us to be involved in educating people without feeling any shame, indignation or fear."

On August 17, 1995, he gave two recommendations for people: "Rest is very important because it is what helps the mind and body relax. Rest is an absolute priority for functioning well and clearly. There are different ways to relax. Sometimes, deep breathing exercises can help relax the mind and body, and they can be done anywhere." He added, "Watching over our health is one of the most important things—eating properly and on time is very important. Almost always, it is all about a good diet plan. . . . If a person is sedentary, they should adjust their diet to that reality. . . . But being disciplined is a must."

He never failed to analyze Puerto Rico's colonial administration, and on August 27, 1995, characterized Puerto Rican Governor Pedro Rosselló's term of office (1993–2001) thus:

> Rosselló's government is set up to help the large corporations, which means that working people and small businesses carry the tax burden—money that is needed for the government administration. The big corporations tell Rosselló what to do. If we look closely, most of the legislation his administration has produced has all been to benefit the rich. And if the rich don't pay taxes, who is going to pay them? Those who cannot buy a colonial administration will. The workers and owners of small businesses will. Rosselló, in his eagerness to make Puerto Rico a state, has promoted a series of bills that essentially make the island operate as a state would. He knows that the majority of Puerto Ricans refuse and reject statehood. He is taking advantage of his power as Governor to speed up the process without caring about the fact that the people said no. The most harmful thing is that his bills go against the best interest of the Puerto Rican people.

Oscar used every opportunity to share his insights on art, politics and imprisonment. On February 9, 1995, he wrote, "i completed a drawing of Belize's Pájaro Grande (Big Bird). It is a species that was almost extinct, but with a good conservation program they have been able to save it." He made sharp comments regarding the efforts made toward his release. Describing himself as "one of those people that believe that there are good things that come out from every bad experience,"[2] he added, "i can see that the release campaign is having some impact . . . i can notice a change in the prison guards' attitude. This means that what has been done is having some results."[3] However, as an experienced community organizer, he pointed out,"i believe that those who are involved in the campaign should become more

[2] March 16, 1995.

[3] July 19, 1995.

involved in reaching all of those who want to offer their support. There is no substitute for door-to-door work in order to reach all the people."[4]

In a letter written on October 1, 1995, he used Congressman Luis Gutiérrez's visits to Puerto Rico as an example, stating that they made an impact.

> What is missing is a more organized campaign that can take advantage of the interest produced by these visits. i believe that what we need is a door-to-door and face-to-face campaign. As long as people are hearing about us, there will be interest. But it will be lost if there is no work to give authenticity to Gutiérrez's statements. People have to be visited. An environment where we have a presence within the people has to be created. If people see that there are some who are doing support work, most will offer their support as well. People identify themselves with things they know—the only way people are going to get to know us is if the campaign gets to involve all the people. And the only way we can do that is if someone goes door-to-door and face-to-face.

He rejected a campaign based on weeping and wailing because "the truth is that lamentations are only good for paralyzing people."[5] And he warned against cynicism and opportunism: "Cynicism stunts the spirit and the will to struggle and resist. . . . [We must] never create opportunities for those who don't use reason and are blinded by hate to get away with their dirty moves."[6]

On May 16, 1995, he criticized the fact that some of his recommendations had been ignored, particularly in the case of Marion: "i had asked you keep focused on political principles. If the emphasis had been in that area, at least people would have had a better appreciation of the conditions at Marion and why the prison guards wanted to keep me there." In April, of that same

[4] October 1, 1995.

[5] February 20, 1995.

[6] April 16, 1995.

month, he pointed out the pending visit of a Catholic religious leader and its significance:

> [The Catholic leader's letter to me] was meaningful because it was the first time since we were incarcerated that the Catholic Church showed interest in our situation. It seems that the transfer to this dungeon has moved some people. Although the jailers did not want that, the first time CNN interviewed me, i was filmed in shackles and handcuffs. Several people who saw the report in Puerto Rico (some within the Catholic church) were deeply affected. i hope that if the visit is accomplished, it will help to start establishing ties between Puerto Rico's Catholic Church hierarchy and us. Its support could have great impact on our people and could help with our release . . . because prison guards have a certain respect toward religious activists.

Prison conditions occupied a great part of his letters' content. He kept his family apprised of his real situation—it was part of the memory that must never be forgotten. As he narrated on February 20, 1995:

> Since i arrived, things have gotten worse. The officers are in all their glory because what is published about this place only covers the official line that they tell the media, and the latter have no interest in what is happening to the inmates. On the contrary, maybe they would like to hear that the conditions are harsher than they are because it would be more sensational

On March 30, he also recounted evolutions in the prison routine:

> Last week a new process to perform the night count was established; now they do it as in Marion and other prisons. On Friday, for the first time since i arrived here, i got to sleep for almost six hours. i was only

woken up three times. On Saturday morning i felt like a new person. But whenever the guards do something positive, they also do some bad things. Since Saturday they started to require that i have to strip if i want to come out of my cell. So as of today, Tuesday, it has been six days since i last went out. Today, they also transferred me to another cell. They put me in a cell that was previously occupied by a man who is insane. The walls were covered with mucus, there was old food on the floor and it reeked of urine. i had to use toothpaste and shampoo to clean the walls, the floor, the shower, and the bed. Since they grab everything you own and put it in the cell, i had to clean everything bit by bit—i moved things from one place, cleaned it, and then moved something else. i am sure the officers moved me to this cell because they knew the hygiene conditions were horrible. The toilet is the worst. They refuse to let me use a brush. i have to figure out a way to clean it. i still haven't been able to fully clean it. So, they let me sleep better, but they also went out of their way to harass me.

They're not too happy with me because many people called (he is referring to the protest campaign regarding his prison conditions). One officer told people i was a liar. But if i was lying, why did they change the night count process so drastically? Before, they did it every half hour. Now, they do it every two or three hours. The difference is like day and night.

On May 10,

they "transferred me" to another unit. Here, i have access to fresh air. Cells have only one door and are not tightly closed. i come out of my cell to eat meals with a group of six people. i'm not subjected to so many strip searches. And i can socialize with other inmates. We are a total of eighteen inmates. The unit has two floors. When i come down to eat, i can speak with the inmates of the first floor. Doors have a small hole through which you can speak. In my floor, i also have enough room to eat. i go to visits with a khaki

> colored outfit. So it is very different, especially because i don't feel the isolation i felt in the other unit.[7]

Seventeen years later, in April 2012, Oscar explained the significance of this first transfer: "The transfer to the new unit was the first step to start the pretransfer program. i had to remain in that unit for eight months, infraction free. But the program was accelerated and in less than five months i had already gone through the two units required to be placed in the last unit. The whole program was completed in 23 months rather than the 44 to 48 months required for a transfer."

Returning to his letters from the era of his transfer, one can see both the swiftness of his progress to less restrictive units and his appreciation for the less dehumanizing conditions there: "During the following weeks the officers will open a second of three units. According to the unit manager, he recommended me for this unit. You have to be there for four months and then you go to the last unit, where you have to stay for a year. He hasn't said anything to me yet about working in the factory, so i don't know what will happen."[8]

A month later, he reflected:

> Well, i've been without cuffs for one month and the truth is that now i can appreciate how harmful they are. i am not exaggerating when i say that cuffs are torture instruments. When you are cuffed with your hands behind your back and the prison guard grabs the cuffs, (they sometimes pull on them and twist them while they walk with you) they pinch your skin and cut off your circulation. After so many years of being handcuffed almost every day, my wrists now feel relief.[9]

After almost ten years in isolation, the prison system finally seemed to allow him to return to a less-isolating prison:

---

[7] May 25, 1995.

[8] Oscar refused to work for military industries. July 19, 1995.

[9] August 27, 1995

> [Finally], they moved me to the last unit of the program. According to the jailer in charge, what he wants is for us to complete the program and be transferred to another prison. i have to spend a year in this unit. On Wednesday they assign us work. i have to work half a day. It's supposed to be a chair factory. The jailers have not told me if they are going to force me to work in their factory. But i will know this week. Here, i'm going to the dining room to eat. i'm with seven other prisoners. It's been many years since i ate in the dining room. These are small changes, but you can appreciate them. In the afternoon, after dinner, i have the option of staying in or out of the cell. If i stay in the cell, they lock me in. It could be that later they will leave the doors open. That's nothing serious for me because i'm always busy doing something in the cell.[10]

Along with thirteen other prisoners, Oscar completed the year required for transfer from the Administrative Maximum (ADX) prison in Florence, Colorado, to another prison. They were all given the option of selecting the prison to which they wished to be transferred, except for Oscar, who was sent back to the prison at Marion.

Why were all the other prisoners who completed the transfer program assigned to the prison of their choice, while Oscar was denied? Why the unequal treatment? Why return him to Marion, the prison most criticized for its persistent violations of human rights? Oscar's answer:

> The decision of the jailers to return me to the gulag at Marion is a crass injustice with a punitive and vengeful purpose. Punitive because the conditions at Marion are now worse than when they took me out in '94. Three recreation areas have been eliminated—the gym, the yard and the handball court. Those were the areas the prisoners that jogged used the most. They substituted with a small space (a cage), surrounded by wire and a cement floor with barely enough space

[10] October 1, 1995.

> to walk. They put 30 prisoners there, together, for recreation. The conditions in the cells are worse. Because the light is opaque and you never get any sunlight, i have to strain my eyes to read. The contaminated water and the noise of the fans stay on 24 hours a day. The reduction in recreation space and the elimination of lights of greater intensity contributes more to the sensory deprivation. Another area that has worsened is the food. i have not seen worse food since i've been imprisoned.
>
> Vengeful because those that made the decision to transfer me here were not the jailers at ADX Florence but the ones in charge of the Regional Office. The jailer at ADX Florence that signed the transfer papers told me, before he left to run another prison in Texas, to be very careful because there were jailers higher up than him that wanted to kick my ass. Why did they want to kick my ass? i believe they are the same jailers that moved to entrap me at Leavenworth and that today enjoy working in the higher levels of the Federal Bureau of Prisons (BOP). They are responsible for the decision.
>
> This injustice has to be attacked. Because an injustice that is not attacked and eradicated is like a cancer that moves and spreads.[11]

The prison at Marion is an appalling institution, condemned by all human rights organizations. Worse than in previous years, Oscar describes it thus:

> In an article written by newsman Alan Prendergast, a jailer from ADX Florence states that now that Marion is a lower security level prison and its mission changed, my transfer here should mean more privileges for me. i have spent a month and a half in this dungeon, and i have been submitted to the same program as before. i'm locked in the cell over 22 hours a day. My hands are cuffed every time i come in direct contact with the jailers. i have no contact visits. i have

[11] December 3, 1996.

three 15 minutes phone calls a month. i have no access to any educational program or any library services. i go out to get fresh air for two hours twice a week as long as the weather permits and the jailers are willing to take me out of my cell. What privileges are these?

The last fourteen months i spent in ADX Florence i could remain outside the cell from 6:00 a.m. to 9:30 p.m. That means that just in one day in Florence i could be outside the cell for more time than was permitted here in a week. There i would go to the dining room for each meal. i would go to the commissary to shop. i would go to the visiting room without being handcuffed. And between September 1995 and November 1996, i went to the hospital twice. Once i had chest x-rays taken by a woman. And the other i went to see the dentist. i was escorted by just one guard and i was never handcuffed.

Two weeks ago i was taken to the hospital here, to take x-rays of the colon using the barium enema. The jailers put the black box and the chains on me. Upon arrival at the hospital, the radiology technician asked the jailers to remove the handcuffs, because i had to take off my clothes and put on a robe. The jailers said that they could not take off my handcuffs unless the lieutenant gave them permission. They called him and he told them what they had to do. They cuffed my legs and while one held me the other took off my handcuffs. i took off my shirt and put on the robe. They put on the handcuffs again and removed the ones on my legs. With my hands cuffed i had to do a Houdini to take off my shoes and the rest of the clothes. They laid me like that on the x-ray table, they inserted a tube in my anus and began the barium enema procedure.

For almost an hour they moved me from one side to the other to take the x-rays. At the end, the jailers repeated the same moves with the cuffs.

If this is a lesser security prison and i'm supposed to have more privileges, then how do you explain cuffing me, making me wear the black box and the chain to get x-rays taken? Where is the privilege in being submitted to this dehumanization and such painful experiences? One has to remember that in 1990 The National Interreligious Task Force on Criminal Justice found that Marion was a prison where they carried out legalized torture.

If the prison at Marion has changed its mission, the program that i'm submitted to reflects no such change. On the contrary, it is worse now than it was in 1994 when i was transferred to ADX. At least then i could go to the gym, the handball court, and to the yard to run. Now the so called "outside recreation" is done in a cage. The interesting thing about the cage is that it's made of concrete and surrounded by barbed and razor wire. What this means is that the construction of each recreation cage adds more security to the prison and denies the prisoner the use of the gym, the area for playing handball and the yard. For me, since i like to run, to deny me the use of these places is a punishment. If the 34 prisoners are walking together in the cage, we can barely move.

One important detail about the program here is that to complete it i have to work in the factory. For 8 1/2 years i refused to work in that place because what they manufacture is cable for the U.S. armed forces. In ADX Florence i agreed to work because what they made there were chairs, and my task was to enter it all in the computer. If i refused to work for 8 1/2 years, i am even less inclined to do it now. So i will spend the rest of my time in prison drinking the dioxin-contaminated toxic water every day—a very dangerous carcinogenic substance. Since the average time that the prisoners spend here is 3 1/2 years maybe the dioxin hasn't affected them that much. But i've already been here 8 1/2 years.

Perhaps there is nothing that better shows how deleterious the situation is here than that of a prisoner requesting the court to sentence him to death. He needs psychiatric treatment and they won't give it to him here. He tells the court that he does not want to get out (his sentence is up in 3 years) because he knows that if he doesn't get the treatment he needs he will commit the same acts that put him in prison.

In a visit that the psychologist made to his cell he was told that he was receiving the best possible treatment under the circumstances. In order to interview him or have a consultation in the hospital with him, they would have had to bring him cuffed with the black box and the chain, and two jailers from the escort would have to be present during the consultation. But while they did the interview in the cell, all the prisoners could hear the conversation. If the mission of Marion has changed, and it is a lesser security prison, why is this prisoner denied the treatment he needs? Why do they have to take such drastic measures that would push him to request that he be put to death in order to get attention?

Anyone alleging that it is a privilege to be here has to be a foolish person with a twisted mind that has been subject to bestial treatment. What else can you expect from a jailer?[12]

How did Oscar respond to the new outrage by the jailers?

What do i propose to do? The only thing at hand and that i can do without complications is to go on a fast. There is nothing in Bureau of Prisons policies that forbids fasting. i don't know how much time the body will last, before the jailers realize what's happening. They can force feed me and put me in segregation. But even so they can't stop me. i believe i can keep fasting and force the jailers' hand. What considerations should i keep in mind? My main consideration is to see if what i do adversely affects the release campaign efforts.

What is required for the fast to work? The main thing is how the outside support campaign is organized. i believe that after the elections, the independence movement suffers from the doldrums. There is nothing in the agenda mobilizing the people. This tells us that it is the right moment to organize support. The lethargy and inactivity can help a lot. You

[12] December 13, 1996.

can push the people outside to fast with me. You can link it to the status situation. Here you can deflate any PNP effort. We could demand that Clinton commit to our release as a good-faith first step.

The pattern of the Clinton administration is to respond when there is a crisis. We have to ask ourselves, how can we create a crisis so he'll deal with the status issue? i believe that if you correctly organize a fasting campaign, we can generate sufficient attention. Soon the 1998 centennial anniversary of Puerto Rico's status as a U.S. colony will be upon us. It is a critical date and if we start to do something concrete, the crisis can occur. Although we can't anticipate what will happen, we do know that it is only through organized action and effort that we will force something to happen.

It is the government that has decided to commit injustices. But it is up to us, the ones being affected, to do something. If i don't do what i have to do, i will have failed my duty. So i prefer to put my health at risk rather than accepting the jailer's injustices. My health is at risk anyway. Part of their purpose is to cause the greatest possible harm to my health. And i'm willing to risk my health in exchange for the U.S. government starting to deal with the issue of the status of Puerto Rico. i'm willing to risk my health in exchange for the U.S. government committing to end its practice of colonialism.

i would like every comrade to respond to my proposal. i'm not asking anyone to fast or to participate in the effort. Although i believe that if one fasts for a day in solidarity, that would help a lot. The sooner you share your ideas, the better. There is time. i think that in a couple of weeks everyone should have responded. The fasting and the solidarity generated should be an effective action and practice. If all goes well, i would like to begin on a significant date: Christmas, Three Kings' Day, De Hostos day, or the day of Clinton's inauguration. i need to hear as soon as possible from the people in charge . . . because the work will be in your hands.[13]

[13] December 3, 1996.

On December 15, 1996, Oscar wrote:

> My decision is not an act of desperation. If i'm going to do something, i don't want it to be an exercise in futility. For the moment i believe that it is important that people understand why i think it's necessary that i take action. i believe that when you confront adversity with positive measures, it can be transformed into something beneficial. Since the transfer to Marion affects me the most, it's up to me to act. i won't do it if it's going to affect the campaign or the comrades negatively.
>
> From my point of view, my proposal will not harm but can help. Because i see it as an exquisite invitation to action. All my comrades can participate as well as the people out there. If the support and solidarity comes through, it would be very concrete.
>
> It appears to be the right moment for action. The lethargy of the independence movement is obvious. The wearing down produced by the electoral campaign every four years is occurring again. In '96, the "issue" that picked up speed and produced some results was the campaign for our release. And i don't think the independence movement leaders are very willing to work on the Campaign. We are also seeing some of the Clinton policies more clearly. His appointment of Bill Richardson as U.S. ambassador to the UN is something that could be positive for us. If we can initiate positive action in the Puerto Rican diaspora to pressure the UN ambassador, that might push him to deal with our reality.

The jailers did not stop seeking revenge against Oscar.

On February 17, 1997, Oscar was operated on at the prison hospital in Springfield, Missouri for a hemorrhoid condition. His mother had passed away three days before.

He wrote:

> i was operated on Monday before noon and that night i was already feeling feverish. Wednesday around 2:00

p.m. they took my temperature and it was at 102.7 degrees. i had never felt a fever like this.

About a half hour later a nurse came accompanied by a guard. i got up and she said she wanted to take some blood. My body was shaking like a hammock, but i did everything possible and she took the blood. Around 15 minutes later they returned and told me they had lost a needle in the cell. i got up again and told them i hadn't seen anything. i helped them look, but the truth is that if she lost a needle, it wasn't here. They left. About a half hour later the guard came with a man. My body was burning up. i got up again. i told them the same thing. The guard said he did not hear anything fall.

Friday they released me from the hospital and returned me to the hole. The jailers that took me were racing wheel chairs. Every turn made me feel as if someone was cutting me with a razor. i got to the cell and was preparing to clean up the blood. A lieutenant came in and said they were going to cuff me. They cuff me, take out of the cell and take me to the area were we shower. He says he wants me to get naked because i stole the needle. When i opened my mouth and started to tell him of the abuse they were committing and the game they were playing, the lieutenant presented his theory. According to him i had stolen the needle and immediately passed it to an accomplice who took it away.

i told him i had a fever of 103°, barely able to move. i don't know anyone, and the whole time there was a guard in front of the room guarding it. But they came up with this diabolic theory 48 hours after the incident. They searched me from head to toe. Blood was running down my legs, and here he was passing a metal detector on my rear. To punish me, they did not allow me to use the sitz bath or give me medications. It wasn't until Saturday morning when a guard who has acted right came and did me the favor of calling the nurse. It wasn't until 10:00 p.m. that they gave me the sitz bath and the antibiotics.

> i don't know why i got such a fever. i know that an infection spread in the area where i was operated on from the day of the operation. Although i tell them that the infection was in the anus, they insist that it is the bladder, the urinary tract. i asked them for medication for the fever and they thought i wanted drugs for the pain. In their twisted minds what they think is that you are getting operated on to get high. i would tell them that the fever and the pain are not related.[14]

More recently, Oscar clarified:

> After the surgery, all i could feel was discomfort. Apparently the surgery had been a sloppy job. A few hours later, my body was in pain and feverish—i knew an infection was setting in and i informed the medical staff about it. i told them i didn't want any pain killers. Yet they injected me with the drugs. The next day, i felt worse and again i was injected with pain killers. The third day the temperature was very high and my body was trembling. i could hardly stand up. And i had not been able to use the toilet because the pain killers had constipated me. Finally the doctor ordered me to be given antibiotics as i had requested the first day. An hour later, my body responded and i was able to use the toilet—an incredibly painful ordeal.[15]

The jailers' brutality still didn't end. It was reflected even in the smallest detail: "i'm writing with a small piece of pencil, about two inches long. It's very difficult to write with something so small. But we have to understand that the mind of a jailer is very twisted and full of nonsense."[16]

In spite of all the daily harassment, Oscar did not lose sight of the possible participation of the prisoners in the solution of the great problems of Puerto Rico:

---

[14] Letter, February 1997.

[15] Letter with reflections, February 2012.

[16] February 19, 1997.

That is why time is of the essence—to declare with more clarity and specificity about the campaign orchestrated by the federal officials to destroy and criminalize us. In the video of the Young Lords and Yoruba Guzmán's book we see how far that campaign went. Why not cite something from that experience? Why not cite the bombing on January 11, 1975 at Hostos's birthday memorial in Mayagüez? Why not cite the grim role of the federal authorities in the frame-up and killing of two young independentistas at Cerro Maravilla? Is it that Puerto Rican lives are not worth anything?

The destruction and criminalization campaign was very effective. And those at the head of it were the federal officials in the Department of Justice.

It's not that we pretend to justify our existence and struggle but to place the responsibility for the facts where they belong. The memory of our pain is worthy of appreciation, remembrance, never to be buried. i saw the destruction (not self-destruction, as some say) of the Young Lords as a result of the dirtiest, most nefarious campaign imaginable. How did the drugs get there, how could they put loved ones to fight against one another, and how was a paranoia created that no one understood? Hundreds of youth were destroyed, but there is not one person imprisoned for that destruction. We can say that some policemen were brought to justice, but who is really responsible for the patterns of criminalization against Puerto Ricans fighting for freedom?

This is not about stirring up old wounds, but to put a particular reality into perspective. Why has the U.S. government been able to cause so much harm for almost one hundred years of colonialism without assuming the least responsibility for what was done? How can that same government maintain a pretense of democracy when political prisoners are held, with no process to deal with the status situation? Said participation is important: not because we are important as individuals, but because we have made a contribution to our people.

> Our contribution is significant. We can see it in the Diaspora, in its neighborhoods and in universities. You can feel it because it has endured three decades while under constant attack. It's important because although not all of us were born in Puerto Rico, no one has been able to tear our Puertorriquenidad from our hearts and minds. We have earned a place in the struggle to eradicate colonialism once and for all. To be included in the process also helps us to have a presence in the everyday occurrences of the people. Perhaps it will be clearer to say that to demand that we have mass participation helps to build our presence and the campaigns for our release.
>
> Those of us who have defended our homeland have paid a high price by affirming that Puerto Rico is a colony. It seems to me that it would be an insult not to defend the idea that we prisoners be included or that we be released as part of the process.[17]

Oscar's captivity in Marion did not diminish his political awareness. He affirmed:

> For over a hundred years it has been the independence movement that has formulated the concept of our political reality, always asserting that we are a colony. Against sea and storm, paying the price of persecution and criminalization, independentismo has affirmed, and reaffirmed, that Puerto Rico's political status is that of a colony. It is an irrefutable truth for everyone who loves justice, freedom, and truth. Today we see that even right-wing politicians and PPD [Partido Popular Democrático] members affirm that Puerto Rico is a colony. Their motives are different, but the truth has prevailed. It has prevailed because we have been unwilling to allow ourselves to be silenced by persecution and criminalization.
>
> If we want to create a just and democratic process for resolving the colonial problem of Puerto Rico, the political prisoners and prisoners of war must be given

[17] February 9, 1997.

the opportunity to participate in it. And that requires our release from prison. We are calling for something that most Boricuas would understand and be willing to support. This is the best way to force the hand of the politicians. Clinton had no problem asking Israel to meet some of the demands of the Palestinians—the most difficult of which was the release of the political prisoners. If this was the case, then he should not have problems accepting a call from the Puerto Rican people that demands our release as part of the process to resolve our status. It is always incumbent on us to define ourselves and formulate our conceptions of our political reality. The issue of our political status cannot be an exception.

i believe that it is necessary to begin to democratize the sacrifice. Our homeland belongs to all those who love it. And if we want to see it be free, then it is up to all of us to struggle for our freedom. Nobody is going to give it to us . . .

We have lived the terror of colonialism. i remember when i used to stop at Armitage and Halsted (two streets in the Puerto Rican section of Chicago), and i would see the faces of many Puerto Rican youths, filled with life, their eyes bright with hope. But six months later, i would only see pale faces and vacant eyes. The terror of drugs had sucked the life out of them. Maybe we didn't go through the ferocious terror that Latin Americans at the high pint of the colonial era suffered. But the results are the same . . . The enemy always prefers to use other colonized people to attack those who resist colonialism. That way they make the issue seem to be one between Puerto Ricans.

i will fast on April 4 and 5 wherever i am. i will do it in solidarity with the compatriots who have, like me, served for 17 years in prison. i will do this to commemorate the death of Martin Luther King, Jr., and to call for our release so that we are given the opportunity to participate in the process of eradicating colonialism. i want this to be left very clear.

Well, take care. We know that we will triumph because sooner or later, the truth prevails.

> Independentismo can claim a victory because it was the only force that dared to affirm that we were a colony. And Puerto Rico will be free because not even annexationism, no matter how strong, can eradicate the reality that we are a distinct people. We will continue pa'lante like Mita—that tomorrow may be better than today.[18]

When Oscar's mother died on February 14, 1997, U.S. authorities had denied him permission to attend the funeral, although friends and families were willing to pay all the travel and lodging expenses that the guards who accompanied him would require. Oscar reflected,

> That same day, they let me call to Puerto Rico. i spoke with my sister and the most painful news i have received since my capture was waiting for me. That afternoon, my mother had died. For my whole family, my mother was the fountain of energy, hope, and faith, where we all went to reinvigorate ourselves. She was a woman full of love, strength, and creativity. She never stopped struggling for us. Sadly, she spent her last years suffering from Alzheimer's—an illness that robbed her of her memory and health. But she bequeathed us with the most virtuous and glorious example a mother can give her children, grandchildren, and great-grandchildren.[19]

The following is a fragment of a thought of Oscar's dedicated to her:

> Decades have passed
> Your spirit has remained free
> No more any chains
> Now just the example
> of a woman who could
> with the love of a mother

[18] March 12, 1997.

[19] February 19, 1997.

give life to many lives
with her sensitivity
converted suffering
into an immunity
that softened the pain
and thus persevered
creating homeland and family.

Through his letters, Oscar provided a most personal account of his second confinement in Marion: "The situation here goes from bad to worse. Not only have two of my drawings disappeared, but they are also messing with my mail. The jailers are responsible for the cancelation of two magazine subscriptions that were paid for one year. They open my legal correspondence and i suspect that they return letters to people."[20] And: "A special visit i recently received from a Puerto Rican political leader was classified as a social visit. But the shamelessness of jailers does not stop there. Since the visit was considered a social visit, it was recorded and put on video. This means that they wanted to hear everything that we talked about and, at the same time, they wanted to force a very limited communication with my visitor."[21]

Protests demanding that Oscar be provided essential medical services and the improvement of prison conditions increased and seemed to have some effect, as he himself observed:

> On November 18, the jailers moved me to another unit. It seems that the protests caused Washington to give them orders to move me. Here i have access to the yard four times a week and an extra phone call per month. i eat my meals outside the cell, in a common area with other prisoners. Therefore, i am locked in the cell less time. i estimate that i spend about 3 1/2 hours a day outside the cell. The jailers have not yet told me what they are going to do with me or what they expect from me. i do not know if

[20] June 26, 1997.

[21] August 27, 1997.

> after a little while here they will put me in the hole as they did in 1990. Let's see what happens and what stories they come up with.[22]

But again, on May 3, 1998, he reported, "The harassment continues . . . it seems that these jailers do not know what else they can do to harm me."

Oscar maintained his resistance. His commitment to independence, the memories of those who have sacrificed themselves for the cause of independence, his family ties, and the voices of his people (which seem to grow increasingly louder with time), served as his support.

He reminds us, "The work and defense of independence needs to be born from the will and conscience of the individual. It cannot be an imposition. It cannot be something you are being obliged to do. Nor is it a question of convincing."[23] And:

> No one can deny how criminal and harmful the invasion and military occupation were. All people aspire to their freedom and to enjoy their sovereignty—ours was usurped. All people aspire to self-determination, but colonialism is the negation of self determination. All people need their own identity, but in our case our citizenship was seized and replaced with a sham U.S. citizenship. It is such a sham that Puerto Ricans in Puerto Rico are not represented in the three branches of government (executive, legislative and judicial) which are the cornerstone of citizenship. The worst thing is that Puerto Ricans have to pay a blood tax because they have to serve in the U.S. armed forces, even though we only have a sham citizenship.
>
> We Puerto Ricans have lived a century of ideological violence. We are criminalized if we love our homeland and want to ensure the common good. That ideological violence is used in Puerto Rico and outside Puerto Rico. What accompanies such a

[22] November 30, 1997.

[23] February 24, 1998.

> serious crime is the depravity of colonialism. That century of corruption has done so much damage that we feel so powerless and weak we cannot even believe we can be free. We accept a lifestyle controlled by fear.[24]

Referring to that fear, he mentioned that on Christmas Eve he received a letter from some friends with whom he had no communication for twenty-five years. In examining the situation, he joyfully noted:

> The good news is that, as friends, they have extended their arms in friendship to break over 25 years of not being in contact. In addition, what strikes me the most is that, for many years, they lived with the fear that the government would retaliate against them if they communicated with me. They already broke the barriers of fear. They taught me that they have more courage than some of my Puerto Ricans friends that are still afraid of communicating with me.[25]

The memory of the heroes of the past encouraged him to continue his struggle. He was very happy that the supporters of the independence movement and past struggles still continue celebrating key commemorations today.

> Now that i have been imprisoned these years, i appreciate the great sacrifices of former Puerto Rican prisoners even more. Many of us complain and do not think of how much people like Andel Rodriguez Cristobal suffered. Seeing how physicians treated prisoners in Leavenworth, and seeing how hard and perilous it is to get sick in prison, i realize first had what great sacrifices people have made. When i arrived at Leavenworth, the same physician who dealt with Nationalist Party prisoner Andrés Figuero Cordero

[24] April 9, 1998.

[25] January 1, 1998.

> was still there; that is the reason why i can talk in detail about how great his sacrifice was. He gave to the motherland with great humility and courage what the vast majority of all of us that consider ourselves patriots are not willing to give. For me, Andrés's birthday has an even greater significance, because that day was the last public activity that Don Juan Antonio Corretjer attended before he died. After returning from Aguada he fell ill and never regained his health.[26]

Written communications allow us to see to what extent the reciprocal affection between Oscar and his family has strengthened Oscar. Neither distance nor the prison bars could separate them. At Christmas of 1997, he said to them, "i hope that you and the whole family there may celebrate Christmas together and have a great time. We must seize the small moments and make them as pleasant and happy as they can be." A few weeks later, he added, "i am glad you decided to celebrate and enjoy Christmas. These are moments that cannot be wasted because time once gone never comes back."

He never forgot to give personal advice: "It is very important that Clarisa and Karina are educated on asthma because when you are well informed you can prevent the disease, you know how to deal with the attacks and what environments affect the person suffering from the disease."[27]

Finally, he always remained concerned about his mother's health.

> Today i watched a story that caught my attention. For some time, i have been hearing that the leaf of the ginkgo biloba tree helps heal the heart. The Chinese have been using it for thousands of years. Now U.S. researchers have found that it helps people who are losing their memory. They have conducted experiments with people that are beginning to suffer from Alzheimer's and have found that it helps them regain their memory. i do not know if it is something that can help Mita. However, i think it is good to know.[28]

---

[26] November 30, 1997.

[27] January 14, 1997.

[28] February 6, 1997.

His unwavering commitment to the freedom of Puerto Rico, family ties, and the voices of the people through the campaign encouraged him, and he never ceased making recommendations.

> i think that next year—until the official July 98 Columbus Quincentennial—the campaign can gain the desired momentum. There are many people waiting expectantly for the one-hundredth anniversary of the invasion, and this may serve as an incentive to win hearts and minds. i think that the campaign can launch another call to Clinton. In recent months, he has said that he wants to be remembered as the president who helped heal the nation. He assumed responsibility for the disastrous and barbaric experiments that the government made with a community of black people who were used as guinea pigs for syphilis research. He also held a conference on race relations. He can also help to heal all the evil that has been done to us with our release. It would be a way to renew sending letters, but this time using what Clinton has declared as his agenda. If his government has perpetrated colonialism for one hundred years in Puerto Rico, and our people have been used as guinea pigs, then he has a duty to do everything in his power to remedy this situation.[29]

The visits from his daughter and his granddaughter renewed his vitality. He had no illusions about his release. However, despite his awareness of the need to limit his thoughts about it, a glimmer of hope filtered through in his words after one of those visits, full of intoxicating tenderness and love:

> Although chances that we will be released from prison are very little, it is necessary that we know what can be done if that becomes a reality. The most important thing is to get to know each other. If i return to Puerto Rico, i do not want to go to the metropolitan area. So i needed to know if she was willing to move out of

[29] June 24, 1997.

> Santurce. It is a matter of urgency that she finish her studies. As more time goes by, it will be more difficult for her. i know that if my release becomes feasible, i have a lot of experience and knowledge that may be useful to her and Karina.[30]

Finally, his willingness to struggle and resist is evident in his simple summary:

> Although there is not much to celebrate here, i always find something positive in my life and i celebrate that. Austrian psychiatrist and Holocaust survivor Victor Frankl used to say that if we do not allow our spirit to succumb even under the most deleterious conditions, we can find meaning in life. Sometimes a very tiny thing turns out to be a meaningful experience.[31]

In 1998, Oscar was transferred to Terre Haute Prison in the state of Indiana. He saw his exit from the gulag of Marion as follows:

> i left Marion with my spirit quite high. i never surrendered to their program as the jailers had wanted me to. i am deeply grateful because you all have given me the necessary support so that the jailers did not achieve all their goals. We do not know all the dirty moves they did, but do not be surprised if one day you discover that they took steps to eliminate me.[32]

He emphasized again the role of the heroes of independence regarding their resistance when he pointed out:

> Don Juan Antonio Corretjer and Doña Consuelo said that one could not fear prison or poverty. i know what poverty is and i know what prison is because i have

[30] Ibid.

[31] January 1, 1998.

[32] August 16, 1998.

> lived them in the flesh. i hope that the only poverty most people fear is spiritual poverty, because the saddest thing is to see people that are poor in spirit (March 16, 2000).

Just before his transfer, he received a visit from an old friend.

> Two days before leaving Marion, i was visited by a friend i had not seen for 27 years. The visit was very good and interesting. The guards could not understand why my American visitor was so excited and even crying. Why are the jailers surprised? This is the third time so far this year that such a thing has happened. i guess it is acceptable for them to see Puerto Ricans excited and showing affection and solidarity, but it's another thing to see an American with blue eyes like theirs do the same. i think that it is the same with the bureaucrats from Justice and the White House. . . .
>
> i think that the decision of my transfer has a dual purpose. One is to try to silence people who supported me. The other is that the Department of Justice—in order to make a negative recommendation to Clinton and look good—believes that it is not to their advantage that there be an example that shows that we have been treated differently from other prisoners. After twelve years of keeping me locked up under such deleterious conditions, an attempt to prolong it even more would make it difficult for the Department of Justice to assert such a thing.[33]

Although conditions at Terre Haute are far from easy, and harassment there has continued in various forms, his long-delayed transfer marked an important victory, as can be seen in this report by his granddaughter, Karina, which reveals both the hardship of his continued imprisonment and the improvement in the conditions there compared to Marion:

---

[33] Ibid.

Our first photograph together was taken in 1998 when he was transferred to Terre Haute, Indiana.

After 12 years in Marion without physical contact, it was in Terre Haute that we had our first hug. When my grandfather stood in front of us, everybody hugged him, except me. I was not accustomed to hugging him because during the previous 7 years I had not been allowed to touch him. So I just did what was my custom, I placed my hands in front him, like I had always done in front of the glass that separated us. My mom is the one who told me that now I could touch him, and then I hugged him. Although physical contact is allowed in this prison, you are only allowed one welcome hug and a goodbye hug.

To enter the visiting room in Terre Haute you have to go through a drug detector known as an ion scan. The problem is that although I am only 14 and I have never done drugs or alcohol, the machine reading has come out positive twice and my visit to my grandfather has been denied. As far as the administration is concerned, the drug could be a cat hair or a prescribed medication. The guards themselves recognize that the machine detects any particle that may be found on your clothing, and that there is a high incidence in which people who stay in hotels or rent cars can come out positive. Unfortunately, I was always taken in rental cars and we stayed in hotels. Now I take my clothes to the dry cleaners and keep it in the plastic until I am ready to use it. I bring my own sheets and towels and the money just the way it was given to me at the bank, and I don't touch anything until the visit.

For the visits in Terre Haute they always seat us in the same area, in front of the guards' desk and all the video cameras in the room. My favorite game is UNO, and each time I go visit I teach him how to play. We try not to laugh so they won't punish grandpa, but we can't help it. While I am with him, I try to make those four hours of visiting time especially wonderful.

Nowadays my Grandfather Oscar calls every week and I try to write him frequently. I visit him several times a year, and I am anxiously waiting for his

> freedom so we can travel and enjoy all the things he has been denied.
>
> I feel very special because two of my grandparents have sacrificed their lives for our homeland. Even though it is something that is very special, at the same time it is something that causes me a lot of sadness and suffering. Our families' sacrifice has been huge, but there is no remorse because it is for a just and noble cause.[34]

Oscar defined the new gulag as the "Terre Haute dungeon" and told us that

> they still have me locked up in the Special Housing Unit, but they have already told me that they are going to place me in general population—[but] not without first giving me certain warnings and making some threats. . . . [35]
>
> However, i am adjusting to the conditions here little by little. It is going to be a slow and difficult process. It is going to be hard to be in a 6' x 9' cell with someone else. There is no privacy. Even getting some sleep is more difficult. The slightest noise affects me. The snoring, the noise someone's nose makes when they have an allergy, even the noise of the bed creaking wakes me up. i know that i will get used to it, but after so many years of being in a cell by myself it is difficult to get accustomed to the new reality.[36]

Painting remained a way of breaking the monotony of the prison routine. He was enthusiastic about it and said,

> It is possible that they might give me a space to paint. It is all tentative. If they allow me to paint, i am going to have to invest around $250.00. i wrote to the

---

[34] Karina Valentín López report to family and supporters, Chicago, 2000.

[35] August 16, 1998.

[36] September 9, 1998.

> Committee for them to help me out with this expense. The money can be recovered fairly quickly by selling just some of the paintings. Although i have not painted with acrylics in quite a while, i am sure that i can make paintings that can be sold.[37]

The jailers knew the liberating effect that painting could have, which is why they persisted in making it difficult. It was not long before Oscar wrote:

> They are placing obstacles on my painting. The supervisor of the Recreation Department told me that he absolutely would not allow me to paint in his area. He gave me some paperwork so that the management of the unit i live in could give me permission to paint. i requested it, but so far they haven't said a thing. For my part, i will continue to fight to get permission to paint because they say they have a painting program.[38]

The oppositional strategies by the jailers failed to intimidate Oscar.

> i am trying to find a way to draw and paint in the cell's small space. i've been working on a drawing but the space is very limited. There are also problems with the lighting. i worked for a couple of hours today, but it was very uncomfortable. i am getting ready for the arrival of the paints.[39]

It is important to understand what being able to develop his painting means for Oscar. It opens a window to create in a place without windows; it is the ability to reaffirm the humanity that is under such constant siege by his oppressors. He explained the significance of being able to carry out this creative work as follows:

---

[37] Ibid.

[38] September 22, 1998.

[39] October 13, 1998.

When i decided to start to paint, i wasn't thinking so much about art as i was about the effects sensory deprivation would have on me after a prolonged lockdown in the Marion prison. i understood the need to integrate and use colors in my routine in order to counteract the effects of being locked up in a 6' x 9' cell for 23 hours a day with no fresh air, no natural light and no access to nature's colors. i was only allowed to go out to the yard for 2 hours a week, and i took advantage of this time to admire nature's wonders.

In the summer of 1990, after realizing that there was no intention of transferring me out of Marion, i spoke with a fellow prisoner who had offered to teach me to paint. He responded positively to my request and helped me fill out the purchase order for the basic materials. The same day i received the materials, right after my first lesson the jailers transferred the fellow prisoner to another unit. This surprised both of us.

With my materials in hand and not knowing what to do with them, i took on the challenge and started to practice daily. i read all the materials i could get my hands on and watched TV programs where they taught drawing techniques.

After 11 months keeping that routine, the jailers declared the paints contraband. i was forced to send all my materials home. From that moment on, they permitted only the use of pencils and pastels. i chose the pastels, and it was the only material i used for the next eight years.

In 1998, when i was transferred to Terre Haute, i was enthused by the idea of being able to experiment with oil paints and paint without any problem. But when i attempted to purchase the oil paints, it was denied. Later, i observed that at least 6 other inmates were using oil paints.

i began to use acrylics. The only space available for painting was inside my own cell, a 6' x 9' space i shared with another prisoner. As soon as i started to paint the harassment began. In the 6 years that i have been here, i am the only prisoner who has had his art materials confiscated twice. The last time they con-

> fiscated them, they placed them in a space with no heating and when they returned them almost all of them were no good. So, in addition to the harassment and not being able to paint for months, i also have to bear the added cost of ruined materials. Paints are not cheap.
>
> During the fourteen years that i have been painting i have learned to appreciate and respect art. During the years i spent in Marion and ADX-Florence, painting helped me to relax and transcend the hostile and dehumanizing environment of the walls and razor wire. It has also helped me to see the world differently and to pay attention to things i used to take for granted. For example, seeing a green leaf during winter, or a butterfly or a grasshopper or a deer in the spring or summer. The challenge was to incorporate all of this into my paintings.
>
> i consider myself a self-taught artist. The art teacher in high school had water paints as a requirement. Since i had no money to buy them, i did the work in charcoal. But the teacher was not pleased and she suggested i should not come back the next semester. At that time, i visualized art the same as tennis, as something that was only for the privileged because they had the money to afford it. In prison, i have understood that is not the case. Unfortunately, i did not have the experience when i was 14 that i had when i entered prison.[40]

His total commitment in favor of independence for Puerto Rico remained the focus of his art and his determination to be productive and active despite imprisonment: "As the die-hard optimist that i am, i believe that independence for our country is viable and that there is no problem we can't tackle and get it resolved."[41] "Working for independence," he noted,

---

[40] Oscar López Rivera, artist's statement for traveling exhibition *Not Enough Space*, Chicago, 2006.

[41] August 16, 1998.

"has to come from the individual's will and conscience; it cannot be imposed. It is not about persuading either.[42]

As the campaigns for the freedom the political prisoners grew in size and stature, Oscar made two important suggestions to help shape the work in the United States and internationally:

> [First], there are people who say they want to work in the campaign, but experience has shown us that when it comes time to roll up their sleeves and get to work, they are nowhere to be found. In spite of that, we have to give them the benefit of the doubt and not reject them. Those who are going to do work are going to do it without having to be invited and without any arm twisting. And those that are all talk and nothing else are going to be exposed sooner or later.[43]

Secondly, he endorsed a very important decision put into practice in Puerto Rico regarding the campaign for the freedom of the prisoners:

> One of the first decisions was to make it nonsectarian, so that people who were not for independence and people who were for independence but did not agree with the actions and politics of the prisoners could participate and collaborate. It was a good decision. And the campaign is neither an exclusive club nor a sectarian cauldron, at least that is what i have been told.
>
> i don't like sectarianism or excluding anyone. In all the work i've done i've never promoted the idea that those who don't share my ideology should be excluded. i can't be accused of being a promoter of sectarianism or exclusivity either in Chicago, New York or Puerto Rico. i worked with people who wanted nothing to do with independence advocates, and i helped people who proclaimed

[42] February 14, 1981.

[43] February 9, 1999.

> themselves mortal enemies of the cause that i had chosen to serve.[44]

In Puerto Rico, the national outcry in favor of Oscar's release from prison further increased. On April 4, 1999, an ecumenical event was held, with the participation of the most prominent figures of the island's different sectors. Father Ángel Dario Carrero, OFM (Order of Friars Minor), vice president of the Conference of Religious Orders, and superior of the Franciscans of Puerto Rico, read his *Boricua Easter Proclamation*, a moving and powerful call to demand the release of political prisoners. The text reads as follows:

> This is the night when all of us Puerto Ricans have chosen to rebuild our mutilated and mutilating memory. It is the time to rescue ourselves from the clutches of oblivion, from the blasphemy of nonsolidarity, from the coldness of indifference and, hopefully, also pull some out from the stench of cruel cynicism. It is time to leave Egypt.
>
> Starting on this holy night, which opens as the day, nobody in the world can ignore the fact that fifteen sons and daughters of this country serve not only their own sentences, but also those of others, their own as well as ours.
>
> It is widely known that they have paid dearly—many times over already—the price for freedom, a price that they never complain about, but rather offer as a sacrifice for our country instead. That sign has fulfilled its purpose, a sign that rises by itself, with its own resurrection force.
>
> Less well-known is the fact that our brothers and sisters have been paying yet another price for quite a while, the price of our indifference before their unjust cross; the price of our coexistence with horror, without being moved by it; the price of our scant and belated struggle for human and civil rights, the price of our increasingly complicit silence; the price of

[44] Ibid.

our ideological blindness to the evidence of torture and death. The sentences are prolonged in the same measure as our ethical awareness is delayed. We are blessing a slow death sentence with our false legal and political arrangements.

It is not only the prisoners who must return home, who must be freed so as to close the circle on their historical deed. Each of us must also return to the house of love, the home of truth, the house of freedom and solidarity, to the banquet, the consensus around a common cause, the fraternal common-union, as our friend Antonio Martorell has rubbed in our faces. We Puerto Ricans also live in an exile that reaches our own future. We are dispersed without a sense of family, caged in scripts imposed by the system. We too must also return to the heart of the small, everyday utopias.

And it is, precisely, the prisoners who reveal to us our current condition as expatriates in our own home and they do so—sadly—with the torture they suffer, with the days that they continue being away from their families, with the deathly conditions that serve as their dwelling. . . . The cross—again the cross—reveals to us who we are. Each of our names is populated with executioner's letters, and it is the victims who have the power to decipher us correctly.

They also point out the paths to the new, the unprecedented and the unforeseeable, in the most unexpected ways. For example, one of the political prisoners recently sent a letter to a parishioner, but in reality, he wanted to talk to you, to us, like an obsession our prisoners have to make us relate to each other in favor of life and love. And, to my surprise, in his letter he quoted a paragraph from my recent book, *Puerto Rico: There Is Hope for Your Future*, which states: "The changes our world needs will not come from great deeds, but small, everyday ones. They won't be big words, but soft whispers of life, hardly a rumor of God will sustain us . . . The changes will not be promoted solely on structural levels; together we must channel people's internal change." To close the quote, our Juan

Segarra Palmer asserts in his own words: "The most intimate part of my being says: Amen."

Prisoners not only challenge us with the scandal of the cross, they also blaze trails for us. And I assure you they are not same old well-trodden paths.

Let's go back to the beginning or the end of these words: the cross they carry for their own convictions is a sign of hope and admiration for some and a sign of error for others, but the cross imposed by us must be a cause of scandal and outrage for all. It is good not to confuse things. This scandal should be transformed into a concrete practice of liberation in the most creative and plural forms.

I want to shout with all the voice I have left in me, that that price of ours, paid by the prisoners, ought to be our ache, it should fill us with anguish and rage. I want to proclaim that the price is not just; it is outrageous and cannot be paid with life any longer. I want to proclaim our new collective project: we must take down from the cross those whom we have crucified.

That is why we're here, in recognition that we are all responsible for the disproportionate sentences that fall on the shoulders of the captives every time we remain aloof. The cross is not there for theatricality, but to see ourselves in it. This is the night when Puerto Ricans should finally recognize that our prisoners' case is really ours: men, women, elderly, adults, youth, children. Our own lives are wagered on that cross, the lives of all Puerto Ricans, our hope. And, paradoxically, in this seemingly small struggle the future of humanity itself is at stake. Our prisoners are in this historic hour, the judges of our consciences, of the collective consciousness.

To the degree that we unite, without hidden agendas, in the struggle for the release of the prisoners, we show the depth and veracity of our love for ourselves and for the God of life.

We have to pardon the debts our prisoners did not contract. This starts by remembering a dual perspective: memory of their unflinching dignity and memory of a dignity which is delayed: ours. That double memory should lead us, on the one hand, to recognize—in a spirit of tolerance—the plurality of paths that we Puerto Ricans have a right to in the interest of securing a better future for our nation, and on the other hand, it should lead us to the rescue of our civil responsibility to guarantee those freedoms and raise our voices in protest when they're trampled with all kinds of deathly official excuses.

Those of us here today do not want to continue contributing a greater weight to the cross our prisoners already bear; on the contrary, we want to make that yoke easy, their burden light, we want to be instruments of the resurrection. We do not want this unfair cross which, becoming more cruel over time has sought to become eternal, to be prolonged any longer. We want the Lord's time of grace to be declared. The yobel resonates today, the Boricua jubilee wants to enter our lives: let us pardon our own debt imposed on the prisoners, forgive ourselves so reality can forgive itself too; let us give Puerto Rico a rest from the ideological boxing, the eternal buying and selling; let's liberate our prisoners by liberating ourselves from turning others into victims and betting on its contemplation as a mystery. Let this be our Boricua Easter Proclamation.

The prisoners give us the gift, at long last, of a common cause to unite our Puerto Rican people, divided for so long by petty interests. It is time to weave together our wills concerning the poor, the excluded, the different: workers, teachers, artists, religious, priests, nuns, pastors, bishops, members of all political parties, policemen, farmers, publicists, doctors, craftsmen, businessmen, heads of agencies, merchants, lawyers, academics, journalists, housewives, janitors, engineers, brothers and sisters all. The Puerto Rican political prisoners in United States jails give us their frailty and poverty, all that they have: their own Hour. Let's turn their hour into our hour of collective consensus toward life.

> Brothers and sisters, let us cross the stretch of desert we still have before us, let's get to the promised land of freedom and solidarity, because this is the night.[45]

On August 5, 1999, a commercial film, *Libertad para los nuestros (Freedom for Our Prisoners)*, premiered in 165 of the island's main cinema venues, with the participation of recognized religious and civic leaders, and beloved local artists, advocating for the humanitarian case of the Puerto Rican political prisoners.

On August 29, 1999, the largest demonstration in the history of our nation took place. It was a mass demand for the release of the imprisoned patriots. The multitude included people of all political ideologies, all religions and occupational sectors, and students. The demonstration's outcry and slogans for freedom echoed in the White House. International voices join the outcry, including some Nobel laureates, and from the United States itself. Oscar sent the following message to his people:

> Some decades ago, our community broke the wall of invisibility and silence by which the world had subjugated us. The shout exploded and the explosion gave way to struggle, hope, energy and creativity. The shout rang out, and even through the ghetto walls you could feel the throbbing of the Boricua heart. Thus, you affirmed your identity and demanded justice, respect for your dignity, equal rights, help to resolve the problems that affected you and to eradicate abusive and discriminatory practices.
>
> The all-powerful who held the reins of power, rather than listen to the community and treat it with the sensitivity it deserved, opted to use repression and criminalizing measures to silence it and make it invisible again. They did not know why those people who were supposed to be super-duper happy with the welfare Amerika gave them—that was the stereotypical image that movies such as *West Side Story* had

---

[45] Ángel Dario Carrero, Order of Friars Minor Capuchin, Boricua Easter Proclamation, message for the Ecumenical act in favor of the release of the Puerto Rican political prisoners, Easter Sunday, 1999.

projected about Puerto Ricans—were standing up to fight. They could not explain why the experts (such as the one of the "Melting Pot" theory) had foretold that Puerto Ricans were becoming "Americanized" and mixing with the concoction in the melting pot that was supposed to be American society. For the all-powerful who held the reins of power the solution was to sic the dogs of repression on the community, to force it to become invisible and silent.

Out of this community and its struggle many of us who are now imprisoned emerged. It was there we were shaped and received our baptism in the struggle. We were part of a youth that, with our actions, shattered the stereotypical image of the docile Puerto Rican and/or those who live off others and welfare, and who also managed to see among their members a gang that became a political organization known as the Young Lords.

We learned to fight and the need became struggle and the struggle became need. We were not violent, nor did we allow violence to be used against us or our community. Many of us chose to serve the struggle for our country and everything related to that, including the struggle for the release of the Puerto Rican political prisoners jailed in U.S. dungeons. We also succeeded in making common cause with other just and noble struggles, and that's how the circle of compassion and solidarity expanded.

Today the struggle in that community, just as in all of the Puerto Rican Diaspora, continues. Just as the same repression and criminalization used since the beginning by the all-powerful holding the reins of power, continue. Because the struggle for just and noble causes can't be annihilated. We have the example of the heroic and just cause of the people of Vieques, who have been fighting the American Navy for six decades. It has been suppressed and criminalized. But finally it's managed to prevail, and has permeated the consciousness of the Puerto Rican people. All of Puerto Rico and the Puerto Rican Diaspora demand the United States Navy get out of Vieques.

> We should feel hopeful. The key is to keep fighting until the day our country is free and justice, freedom, participatory democracy and the search for truth prevail. May compassion and solidarity prevail as well, so Puerto Rico can become part of the Universal Homeland.[46]

President Clinton responded to the cries for freedom and granted parole under certain conditions. Explaining his reasons for this action, he said, "They were serving extremely long sentences—in some cases 90 years—which were disproportionate to the offense." He continued by pointing out that "our society believes that punishment should fit the crime. . . . Whatever the behavior of other members of the FALN may be, these petitioners—although convicted for serious offenses—were not convicted for crimes associated with the death or mutilation of any human being."[47]

Eleven of the prisoners accepted the required conditions and were released on September 10, 1999. To qualify, Oscar was required to serve ten additional years of imprisonment. He refused the offer of the president because it was not extended to all of the imprisoned comrades and because he believed that, based on the history of persecutory treatment on the hands of the FBI, the jailers would not allow him to fulfill the conditions successfully. The set-ups and the entrapment to which he had been subjected previously were still fresh in his memory.

His imprisonment in Terre Haute has continued to subject him to systematic harassment and the jailers' efforts to come up with new ways to abuse someone who survived the tortures at Marion. In 1998, when he arrived at Terre Haute's prison, he was placed in a special high-security program, requiring him to present himself before a prison guard every two hours or risk placement in segregation. The captain in charge promised he would be removed from this program after eighteen months of good conduct, telling him, "I am a man of my word." After twenty-two

---

[46] August 29, 1999.

[47] *New York Times*, September 22, 1999.

months, the captain said that there were changes in the program and that he should investigate it, but then the captain was promoted and transferred to another prison. Others made similar promises but never came through; meanwhile, Oscar earned the record for the prisoner who had spent the most time under this type of monitoring, which continues as of this writing (at the end of 2012). In 2005, his Unit Team informed him that he would meet the necessary requirements to be transferred to a lower-security facility, if it were not for this every two hours reporting requirement. In January, Warden Mark Bezy refused to take Oscar off the program, and asserted that the nature of his crime (seditious conspiracy) and the length of his sentence (seventy years) gave rise to "security concerns" which took precedence over Oscar's "good institutional adjustment."

During the last three weeks of January 2006, the Terre Haute prison was in a state of complete lockdown. For Oscar this meant remaining locked in the cell twenty-four hours a day; no phone calls; instead of hot meals, boxed goods which consisted of food with expired dates; access to a shower once a week for ten minutes; no going outdoors; no sunlight. Oscar responded to this:

> i spent over 12 years under similar conditions. . . . i want you to know that i don't care what the jailers do to me. It doesn't matter if they lock me up in a dark hole without access to anything. They will never be able to break my spirit or my will. Every day i wake up alive is a blessing. My duty is to try to use all the time in that day to do something for the struggle of our country and for a better and more just world.[48]

This lockdown was the first of many during 2006.

Oscar's complete lockdown was finally withdrawn the first week of February, 2006. The digestive and sleep problems that resulted from this four-week lockdown began to settle once he was able to resume his normal diet and exercise routine. In that same year, however, his legal mail was being opened in violation

[48] February 2, 2006.

of Bureau of Prisons policy and other mail was retained for long periods of time. Some of his letters did not reach their addressees and there is the suspicion that they were not being sent at all.

In December 2006, his fifteen-year-old granddaughter Karina traveled from Puerto Rico to visit during the Christmas holidays, and the visit was denied. Prison officials argued that the university professor accompanying her showed positive results in a test for contact with controlled substances, as reflected by equipment they had recently begun to use. Although the test was known to be unreliable, generating frequent false positive results, both were refused entry. His daughter Clarisa, and Damian Rodríguez, had received the same treatment in September 1998.

In 2006, the United States undertook several public efforts with several countries to free political prisoners in their respective countries while refusing to consider the release of the Puerto Rican political prisoners, including Oscar, who still remained in their prisons serving a disproportionate sentence, and receiving treatment that violated the international standards regarding the imprisonment of political prisoners.

Since 1990, Oscar has not had any disciplinary incidents, despite the administrative variable that required monitoring every two hours with the purpose of monitoring his every movement. During his imprisonment, he has earned 104 credits from Kansas University and Kansas Community College. He has also worked constantly, even under the most difficult conditions of confinement, receiving high evaluations and earning the trust of the supervisory staff. Finally, he has grown as an artist of deserved recognition and his works have been exhibited in the United States, Puerto Rico, and Mexico between 2005 and 2009.

In 2006, the U.S. Embassy in Mexico tried to stop the exhibition *Not Enough Space* by Oscar López Rivera and Carlos Alberto Torres in the Clavijero Cultural Center of Moreira, Mexico. The exhibit was sponsored by the government of Michoacán. A representative of the State's Ministry of Culture retorted that the exhibition seeks to create awareness of the scarcely known fact that colonialism still exists in the American continent and that the neighbor of the north practices it, which is rarely known due to the control of information. He pointed out that "behind bars, and through the plastic arts, Carlos Alberto and Oscar López have continued fighting for the independence of Puerto Rico."[49]

[49] Ernesto M. Vargas, "Puerto Ricans in Struggle: Not Enough Space Exhibit in the Clavijero," *La Voz de Michoacán*, July 28, 2006.

OUTLOOK FOR THE FUTURE

★

In January 2011, in response to the appeals of family and friends, Oscar applied for parole before the U.S. Parole Board. His application included letters of support from many prominent political figures in Puerto Rico and the United States, and from representatives of various groups within civil society. The request for parole was denied in violation of the most basic judicial principles. Many voices of protest condemned the continued imprisonment of the Puerto Rican patriot and described the decision as an act of revenge by the United States. Resident Commissioner Pedro Pierluisi was among the voices of disapproval. In an official statement he said, "I do not see how anyone can justify 12 more years of confinement after nearly 30 years in prison, especially when the others who were charged with the same conduct are already in the free community. It seems excessive to me."[1] The president of the Puerto Rican Independence Party (PIP), Rubén Berríos Martínez, stated, "It would be despotic, cruel and vile to deny freedom to Puerto Rican political prisoner Oscar López Rivera, held for nearly 30 years in a U.S. prison"[2]

The following testimony, given by Luis Nieves Falcón, on January 5, 2011, joins that opposition:

> On January 5, the day before your birthday and on the eve of Three Kings Day [Feast of the Epiphany], Oscar, I was devastated by the brutal words. They come from far away. Beyond the ocean. Beyond humanity. These words of vengeance and hatred arrived like an intravenous drip, spaced apart in the prolonged torment of torture. They reveal themselves with the coldness of the grave that chills me to the bones. They cut to the heart. Words of abuse that ruthlessly stripped the bare blanket of my body, the fragile storm shutter of my spirit. Offensive words from the oppressors who with cruel laughter relish the pain of my pain. The pummeling, stacked with the words—"Parole denied. Let him serve 15 more years. Let him rot in jail"—proclaims to everyone the Calvary of the brother whom I cannot embrace, though I have arms; whom I cannot see, though I have eyes; whom I cannot speak to, though I have a voice; whom I cannot cry with, though I have tears; whom I cannot comfort, though I have a heart.
>
> He is my brother, Oscar López Rivera. He is my friend, Oscar López Rivera. He is my comrade, Oscar López Rivera. He is no longer present. The chains that clothe his body have forced the distance. The bars that surround his small physical space have forced the distance. However, the vile jailers have not been able to make his absence absolute. Because his presence remains in our hearts. Because his image endures in our minds. The memories of love and affection sustain us both.

---

[1] José Delgado, *El Nuevo Día*, January 6, 2011.

[2] *Inter News Service*, January 7, 2011.

Oscar, my brother. You have been confined for 30 years in hovels where there is not even enough space to stretch out. You have been deprived of visits by those who love you. They have injured your body more than they injured the crucified Christ. You have been denied the right to write and you have had to turn your mind into the blackboard of your daily suffering. But the evildoers who oppress you do not know that the memories keep you alive in the prison of the dead. The memories of those who died, of those who were tortured and imprisoned in Lares and Río Piedras. In Ponce, Jayuya, Utuado, and San Juan. In Hormigueros. Their sacrifice gives you the spirit to survive your martyrdom and withstand the brutishness of the colonial oppressors.

When the horde of murderers believed that they had accomplished your destruction, you reemerged like the glorious moriviví,[3] like the pitirre,[4] an eternal fighter, and reaffirmed your presence as an incorruptible combatant, with dignity. The ever-present dignity of our people.

Oscar, my friend, the terrible ordeal of your imprisonment pains my soul. It hurts so deeply. It surpasses my own physical pain. And, I dream together with you. Together with you I dream the shared hope of a redeemed homeland. A homeland where the blue sky is really the blue color of redemption. Where in a sea of greens, green continues to be the color of liberation.

Oscar, comrade, I suffer with you, cry with you, fight with you. There are no feelings of hatred toward

---

[3] The *moriviví* (Mimosa pudica) is a sensitive perennial plant that withers when touched or shaken to latter revive or reemerge in all its vitality once more. The *moriviví*, whose name literally combines words for death and life, is known in English as "sensitive plant," "humble plant," and "touch-me-not." This shrubby plant has hairy and spiny stems. It has medicinal properties and has been used to treat leprosy, dysentery, vaginal and uterine complaints, inflammations, burning sensation, asthma, leucoderma, fatigue, and blood diseases.

[4] The *pitirre* (kingbird) is a small, maneuverable bird that fiercely defends its territory against invasion by the larger, eagle-like *guaraguao.* The quote alludes to a Puerto Rican saying, "Every *guaraguao* has its *pitirre.*"

> the perpetrators who offend you deeply in jail, and do the same to us here in their external colonial prison. But also, like you, we are confident that our homeland will be free. And that day, embracing in an endless hug, crying tears of joy—because people also weep for joy—with our pain together, sharing our tears, we will be happy because we contributed to achieving peace and happiness for our people.
>
> Oscar, brother, friend and comrade, we follow the same path. The struggle for your freedom is also the struggle for our freedom and our homeland: Puerto Rico. The struggle continues and, you Oscar, you are the road that the Homeland beckons us to follow. Freedom, Peace, Justice. Oscar, my soul brother, you are always present among us. You are always present in our heart. We shall overcome.[5]

The U.S. Parole Board adopted the vile recommendation, which clearly reveal the despotic government's measures to keep the anticolonial fighter behind bars. Their bestial conduct is reminiscent of the entrapments already suffered during Oscar's long imprisonment. Oscar analyzed the situation, and his ongoing communication with his people renewed strength to continue the struggle. In the following public statement, he affirmed:

> From the depths of my soul I wish to express the greatest gratitude to my people for all the support they have given us, the Puerto Rican political prisoners, for more than three decades and, particularly, for their efforts in the current campaign for my release. We have not achieved the desired goal. But we achieved something more beautiful, more precious and more important. And that is the fact that the campaign included people who represent a rainbow of political ideologies, religious beliefs, and social classes that exist in Puerto Rico. This to me represents the magnanimity of the Boricua heart—one filled with love,

[5] "Oscar López Rivera: Brother in the Struggle and Hope," San Juan, Puerto Rico, January 5, 2011.

compassion, courage and hope. That heart allows us to transcend differences and overcome any obstacle when it is a question of fighting against injustice. And it is that heart which makes loyalty and allegiance to my Puerto Rican national identity, to the just cause I chose to serve, and to my indispensable principles beat in my own heart. Why did I apply for parole? Until the summer of 2010, my position was not to apply for parole. But three events at that particular time influenced my decision to change my position. The first was the death of my older sister, who until then had been the cornerstone of the family. And my immediate and extended family asked me to do everything possible to return home. The second was the release of comrade Carlos Alberto. Comrades in the cause urged me to take the step that the comrade had taken. And the third reason was the struggle of the students at the University of Puerto Rico (UPR) that was taking place. It was evident to me that there was a new generation of fighters with the ability, skill, creativity and commitment to relieve the older generation that struggled for decades. What happened with the application? On January 5, there was a hearing with an examiner for the Parole Commission. I was prepared for a hearing more or less similar to the one held for Carlos Alberto. But what I faced was not a hearing but an inquisition conducted by examiner Mark Tanner. The first thing that the jailers did was to handcuff my hands with a black box—something that is very uncomfortable and irritating. Mr. Tanner brought an FBI agent who condemned Clinton at the hearings in the Congress and the Senate for offering parole in 1999. One of them, accompanied by the FBI agent who has tried to harm me the most, delivered the same diatribe he gave before Congress in Attorney General Eric Holder's confirmation hearings. When it was time for my lawyer, Jan Susler, and I to speak, Mr. Tanner assumed the role of inquisitor. His voice turned sarcastic and he never paid attention to what we were saying. After nearly three hours, he ended the hearing and stuck me with the recommendation to see me in

15 years. On February 18, the Parole Commission accepted the examiner's recommendation and decided to deny parole and continue my imprisonment for 15 more years until another hearing is held in January 2026 or to continue in prison until the expiration of the sentence, whichever comes first. I think you need to have an understanding of the Commission's reason for being and what it represents. Almost all members, if not all, were appointed by Bush during his administration. More than two decades ago, the government legislated to abolish it. But like all bureaucracies, it has also taken a life of its own, and has been able to perpetuate itself. Looking at it from that standpoint, we can understand that a decision like the one made in my case extends their life for at least 15 more years. In addition, the Commission is an agency within the United States Department of Justice, which works very closely with two other Justice Department agencies—the FBI and the Federal Bureau of Prisons. They have played down and dirty to keep me in prison for the rest of my life. During the nearly 30 years that I have been in prison, both the Bureau of Prisons and the FBI have committed serious abuses and injustices to harass me and have managed to keep me locked as long as possible. Now what? Since I made the decision to apply, I prepared for the worst. Because I knew that the Commission would not consider my case with a fair attitude, in good faith, and impartially. Since parole is not a right but is classified as a "privilege," it means that the process is at the whim of the commissioners' arbitrariness and subjectivity. And the commissioners are people who advocate an iron fist. Knowing this, we cannot see their decision as a defeat but as another challenge to face. I will appeal the unjust decision of the Commission, fully aware that they are not going to change it. I do this because injustices have to be revealed. Nothing has been or will be in vain. The work that has been carried out is in itself very fruitful. And that work will continue to grow and grow exponentially until we put an end to the injustices that we experience.

I want to take this opportunity to extend the same gratitude to all freedom justice loving people throughout the world who have supported us and continue to support comrade Avelino (alleged member of the Macheteros) and me.

With great respect and humility, thank you. All life is struggle.

In resistance and struggle, OLR[6]

The U.S. Parole Commission confirmed its vindictiveness against Oscar, revealing even more clearly its contempt for justice.

But before us is the image of an unyielding fighter.

He is the symbol:

Nunca podrán doblegar
tu espíritu consistente
que te hace resistente
y difícil de aplastar.
No pueden imaginar
en su innegable torpeza
que eres de noble corteza
nacido en San Sebastián
fuerte como el guayacán
y hecho de una sola pieza.

(They will never subdue
the will of your resolute
spirit that makes you resilient
and difficult to subjugate.
They cannot imagine
in their undeniable ineptitude
that you are of noble lineage
born in San Sebastián
strong like the ironwood
and solid as stone.)
—Juan Camacho, "Oscar López Rivera"

[6] Oscar López Rivera, Letter to my beloved people, Terre Haute prison, Indiana, March 2, 2011.

The best tribute we can extend to Oscar is to continue to fight every day, with yet greater determination, for his release. Every day that Oscar remains in prison is another reminder of the hypocrisy and absurdity of the U.S. government's talk of human rights in light of its colonial rule. In the strongest possible terms, let us raise our voices to denounce this abuse and demand freedom for Oscar López Rivera.

ACKNOWLEDGMENTS

Every book is a collective effort, but this transcontinental edition—birthed by the Puerto Rican movement and its solidarity supports—is a particular example of collective efforts for collective liberation. Therefore, it is appropriate to begin this section of thanks with recognition to the organization formerly headed by Dr. Luis Nieves Falcón, which continues the work for the release of Oscar: the Puerto Rican Committee on Human Rights. Dr. Falcón also wishes to give special thanks to the family members of Oscar who worked to make this book possible: Mercedes López Rivera, Dr. Jose López, and Clarissa López. In addition, special thanks are due to the initial translator of this book, former political prisoner Juan Segarra-Palmer.

The English edition of *Between Torture and Resistance* has been copublished by two U.S.-based organizations, New York's Resistance in Brooklyn (RnB) and the national Interfaith Prisoners of Conscience Project. RnB, an anti-imperialist, anti-racist collective which grew in part out of the work of the Free Puerto Rico Committee and the New Movement for Puerto Rican Independence and Socialism, celebrates its twentieth year in 2012, in part by redoubling its work for the release of all political prisoners. This book and the PM Press book of the collected writings of former Black Panther Russell Maroon Shoatz—still held in solitary confinement after close to thirty years of such inhumane and torturous treatment—are part of that commitment. Funds to assist the publication of this book, and to keep the price low enough so that it can be used as a tool of the freedom movement, were raised in part through the web-based efforts of a Kickstarter campaign. In addition to thanking the good folks of Kickstarter for their support, we offer gratitude to all of those who responded to the call. The first name listed earns that distinction because of the alphabetical placement of names (by first name). Alejandro Luis Molina, however, is more than simply an "A" on our list; his assistance with updating Oscar about the progress of the book, and with getting the entire National Boricua Human Rights Network (http://boricuahumanrights.org) behind the project, has been essential to its success. All supporters, though, merit special recognition: Alejandro Luis Molina, Ana López, Ann Boylon, Barbara Zeller, Benjamin Ramos and Pro-Libertad, Betsy Mickel, Bob Lederer, Bryan Welton, Claude Marks, Dan Berger, Dana Barnett, Diana Crowder, Donna Willmott, Dorothea Elspeth Meyer, Huntley Nieves, Dusty White, Eleanor Kinnear, Elizabeth Fraser, Elizabeth Roberts, Enid Karpeh, Erendira Ramirez, Eve Rosahn, Franklin Collazo, Fred Ho, gabriel sayegh, Geri Almonte, Gloria Alonzo, Gloria Bletter, Graeme Brown, Gregg Peter Farah, Howard Emmer, Jamie Monte, Jesse Heiwa, John Riley, John Weber, Johnnie B. Baker, Jonathan Keller, Josh MacPhee & Dara Greenwald, Juanita Boricua, Kristin Schwartz, Laura Whitehorn, Layne Mullett, Leah Gitter, Lee Carlson, Lilith Rogers, Linda M. Thurston, Louise Kurshan, Margaret Power, Mark E. Mendoza, Mary Patten, Matthew Lyons, Meg Starr & Matt Meyer, Michael Novick, Michael Plant, Michael Staudenmaier, Mickey Ellinger, Miguel Angel Morales, Mikazuki Publishing House, Nanette Yannuzzi-Macias, Nozomi Ikuta, Nuris Rodriguez, Patricia Levasseur, Paul Magno, Perla de Leon, Peter D. Meyer, Peter Vale, Ramon J. Conde, Randy W. Hunt, Raúl Quiñones Rosado, Ray Luc Levasseur, RosieLea, Sarah S. Saul, Scott Campbell, Sean Meyer, Shelley Miller, Susan Kingsland, Susan Scott, Sukey Tamarkin, Suzanne Ross, Therese Coupez, Tibby Brooks, Timothy Schneider, Toby Emmer, Virtual Boricua, William Guzman, and Yeidy Rosa.

We would be remiss in not thanking the ever-patient and hard-working comrades at PM Press—Ramsey Kanaan, Craig O'Hara, Romy Ruukel, and Gregory Nipper among them—and Morgan Buck of Antumbra Design for supporting both the politics and the professional production of this book. Finally, the editors of this volume wish to thank Oscar López Rivera, whose works, paintings, and life inspire us to do much more than work for his release. Oscar inspires us to carry on in the struggle for the complete liberation of all people, showing us that—despite adversity—there is great beauty and strength and victory awaiting us all.

BECOME A FRIEND OF

These are indisputably momentous times—the financial system is melting down globally and the Empire is stumbling. Now more than ever there is a vital need for radical ideas.

In the five years since its founding—and on a mere shoestring—PM Press has risen to the formidable challenge of publishing and distributing knowledge and entertainment for the struggles ahead. With over 200 releases to date, we have published an impressive and stimulating array of literature, art, music, politics, and culture. Using every available medium, we've succeeded in connecting those hungry for ideas and information to those putting them into practice.

Friends of PM allows you to directly help impact, amplify, and revitalize the discourse and actions of radical writers, filmmakers, and artists. It provides us with a stable foundation from which we can build upon our early successes and provides a much-needed subsidy for the materials that can't necessarily pay their own way. You can help make that happen—and receive every new title automatically delivered to your door once a month—by joining as a Friend of PM Press. And, we'll throw in a free T-Shirt when you sign up.
Here are your options:

- $25 a month: Get all books and pamphlets plus 50% discount on all webstore purchases
- $40 a month: Get all PM Press releases (including CDs and DVDs) plus 50% discount on all webstore purchases
- $100 a month: Superstar—Everything plus PM merchandise, free downloads, and 50% discount on all webstore purchases

For those who can't afford $25 or more a month, we're introducing Sustainer Rates at $15, $10 and $5. Sustainers get a free PM Press t-shirt and a 50% discount on all purchases from our website.

Your Visa or Mastercard will be billed once a month, until you tell us to stop. Or until our efforts succeed in bringing the revolution around. Or the financial meltdown of Capital makes plastic redundant. Whichever comes first.

PM Press was founded at the end of 2007 by a small collection of folks with decades of publishing, media, and organizing experience. PM Press co-conspirators have published and distributed hundreds of books, pamphlets, CDs, and DVDs. Members of PM have founded enduring book fairs, spearheaded victorious tenant organizing campaigns, and worked closely with bookstores, academic conferences, and even rock bands to deliver political and challenging ideas to all walks of life. We're old enough to know what we're doing and young enough to know what's at stake.

We seek to create radical and stimulating fiction and non-fiction books, pamphlets, t-shirts, visual and audio materials to entertain, educate and inspire you. We aim to distribute these through every available channel with every available technology—whether that means you are seeing anarchist classics at our bookfair stalls; reading our latest vegan cookbook at the café; downloading geeky fiction e-books; or digging new music and timely videos from our website.

PM Press is always on the lookout for talented and skilled volunteers, artists, activists and writers to work with. If you have a great idea for a project or can contribute in some way, please get in touch.

PM Press
PO Box 23912
Oakland CA 94623
510-658-3906
www.pmpress.org

ALSO AVAILABLE FROM PM PRESS & WAR RESISTERS LEAGUE

We Have Not Been Moved: Resisting Racism and Militarism in 21st Century America
Edited by Elizabeth "Betita" Martínez, Mandy Carter & Matt Meyer
ISBN: 978-1-60486-480-9
$29.95

We Have Not Been Moved is a compendium addressing the two leading pillars of U.S. Empire. Inspired by the work of Dr. Martin Luther King, Jr., who called for a "true revolution of values" against the racism, militarism, and materialism which he saw as the heart of a society "approaching spiritual death," this book recognizes that—for the most part—the traditional peace movement has not been moved far beyond the half-century-old call for a deepening critique of its own prejudices. While reviewing the major points of intersection between white supremacy and the war machine through both historic and contemporary articles from a diverse range of scholars and activists, the editors emphasize what needs to be done now to move forward for lasting social change. Produced in collaboration with the War Resisters League, the book also examines strategic possibilities of radical transformation through revolutionary nonviolence.

Praise:

"When we sang out 'We Shall Not Be Moved' in Montgomery and Selma, we were committed to our unshakeable unity against segregation and violence. This important book continues in that struggle—suggesting ways in which we need to do better, and actions we must take against war and continued racism today. If the human race is still here in 2111, the War Resisters League will be one of the reasons why!" —Pete Seeger, folk singer and activist

"The rich and still evolving tradition of revolutionary pacifism, effectively sampled in these thoughtful and penetrating essays, offers the best hope we have for overcoming threats that are imminent and grim, and for moving on to create a society that is more just and free. These outstanding contributions should be carefully pondered, and taken to heart as a call for action." —Noam Chomsky, professor emeritus of linguistics at the Massachusetts Institute of Technology; philosopher, cognitive scientist, and activist

ALSO AVAILABLE FROM PM PRESS & KERSPLEBEDEB

Let Freedom Ring: A Collection of Documents from the Movements to Free U.S. Political Prisoners
Edited by Matt Meyer
ISBN: 978-1-60486-035-1
$37.95

Let Freedom Ring presents a two-decade sweep of essays, analyses, histories, interviews, resolutions, People's Tribunal verdicts, and poems by and about the scores of U.S. political prisoners and the campaigns to safeguard their rights and secure their freedom. In addition to an extensive section on the campaign to free death-row journalist Mumia Abu-Jamal, represented here are the radical movements that have most challenged the U.S. empire from within: Black Panthers and other Black liberation fighters, Puerto Rican independentistas, Indigenous sovereignty activists, white anti-imperialists, environmental and animal rights militants, Arab and Muslim activists, Iraq war resisters, and others. Contributors in and out of prison detail the repressive methods—from long-term isolation to sensory deprivation to politically inspired parole denial—used to attack these freedom fighters, some still caged after 30+ years. This invaluable resource guide offers inspiring stories of the creative, and sometimes winning, strategies to bring them home.

Praise:

"Within every society there are people who, at great personal risk and sacrifice, stand up and fight for the most marginalized among us. We call these people of courage, spirit and love, our heroes and heroines. This book is the story of the ones in our midst. It is the story of the best we are." —asha bandele, poet and author of *The Prisoner's Wife*

"As a convicted felon, I have been prevented from visiting many people in prison today. But none of us should be stopped from the vital work of prison abolition and freeing the many who the U.S. holds for political reasons. *Let Freedom Ring* helps make their voices heard, and presents strategies to help win their release." —Daniel Berrigan SJ, former Plowshares political prisoner and member of the FBI Top Ten Wanted List.

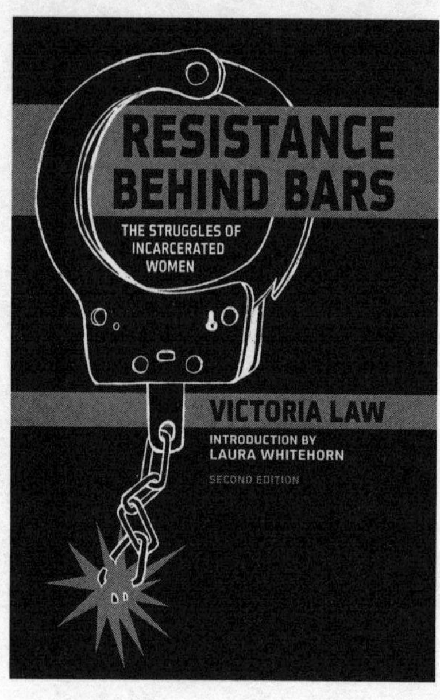

ALSO AVAILABLE FROM PM PRESS

Resistance Behind Bars: The Struggles Of Incarcerated Women, 2nd Edition
by Victoria Law
ISBN: 978-1-60486-583-7
$20.00

In 1974, women imprisoned at New York's maximum-security prison at Bedford Hills staged what is known as the August Rebellion. Protesting the brutal beating of a fellow prisoner, the women fought off guards, holding seven of them hostage, and took over sections of the prison.

While many have heard of the 1971 Attica prison uprising, the August Rebellion remains relatively unknown even in activist circles. *Resistance Behind Bars* is determined to challenge and change such oversights. As it examines daily struggles against appalling prison conditions and injustices, *Resistance* documents both collective organizing and individual resistance among women incarcerated in the U.S. Emphasizing women's agency in resisting the conditions of their confinement through forming peer education groups, clandestinely arranging ways for children to visit mothers in distant prisons and raising public awareness about their lives, *Resistance* seeks to spark further discussion and research into the lives of incarcerated women and galvanize much-needed outside support for their struggles.

This updated and revised edition of the 2009 PASS Award winning book includes a new chapter about transgender, transsexual, intersex, and gender-variant people in prison.

Praise:

"Victoria Law's eight years of research and writing, inspired by her unflinching commitment to listen to and support women prisoners, has resulted in an illuminating effort to document the dynamic resistance of incarcerated women in the United States." —Roxanne Dunbar-Ortiz

"Written in regular English, rather than academese, this is an impressive work of research and reportage" —Mumia Abu-Jamal, political prisoner and author of *Live From Death Row*

ALSO AVAILABLE FROM PM PRESS

Lucasville: The Untold Story of a Prison Uprising, 2nd ed.
by Staughton Lynd
ISBN: 978-1-60486-224-9
$20.00

Lucasville tells the story of one of the longest prison uprisings in U.S. history. At the maximum security Southern Ohio Correctional Facility in Lucasville, Ohio, prisoners seized a major area of the prison on Easter Sunday, 1993. More than 400 prisoners held L block for eleven days. Nine prisoners alleged to have been informants, or "snitches," and one hostage correctional officer, were murdered. There was a negotiated surrender. Thereafter, almost wholly on the basis of testimony by prisoner informants who received deals in exchange, five spokespersons or leaders were tried and sentenced to death, and more than a dozen others received long sentences.

Lucasville examines the causes of the disturbance, what happened during the eleven days, and the fairness of the trials. Particular emphasis is placed on the inter-racial character of the action, as evidenced in the slogans that were found painted on walls after the surrender: "Black and White Together," "Convict Unity," and "Convict Race."

An eloquent Foreword by Mumia Abu-Jamal underlines these themes. He states, as does the book, that the men later sentenced to death "sought to minimize violence, and indeed, according to substantial evidence, saved the lives of several men, prisoner and guard alike." Of the five men, three black and two white, who were sentenced to death, Mumia declares: "They rose above their status as prisoners, and became, for a few days in April 1993, what rebels in Attica had demanded a generation before them: men. As such, they did not betray each other; they did not dishonor each other; they reached beyond their prison 'tribes' to reach commonality."

"There is a temperature at which the welder's torch becomes so hot and burns with such purity that its flame is no longer yellow, orange, or red, but burns blue. Then it is capable of cutting through steel. Staughton Lynd wields the blue flame of truth, cutting through the lies, threats, evasions, and misrepresentations of the authorities of the state of Ohio."—Professor Peter Linebaugh, Department of History, University of Toledo; author of *The London Hanged* and co-author of *The Many-Headed Hydra*

ALSO AVAILABLE FROM PM PRESS

Love and Struggle:
My Life in SDS, the Weather Underground, and Beyond
by David Gilbert
ISBN: 978-1-60486-319-2
$22.00

A nice Jewish boy from suburban Boston—hell, an Eagle Scout!—David Gilbert arrived at Columbia University just in time for the explosive Sixties. From the early anti-Vietnam War protests to the founding of SDS, from the Columbia Strike to the tragedy of the Townhouse, Gilbert was on the scene: as organizer, theoretician, and above all, activist. He was among the first militants who went underground to build the clandestine resistance to war and racism known as "Weatherman." And he was among the last to emerge, in captivity, after the disaster of the 1981 Brink's robbery, an attempted expropriation that resulted in four deaths and long prison terms. In this extraordinary memoir, written from the maximum-security prison where he has lived for almost thirty years, Gilbert tells the intensely personal story of his own Long March from liberal to radical to revolutionary.

Today a beloved and admired mentor to a new generation of activists, he assesses with rare humor, with an understanding stripped of illusions, and with uncommon candor the errors and advances, terrors and triumphs of the Sixties and beyond. It's a battle that was far from won, but is still not lost: the struggle to build a new world, and the love that drives that effort. A cautionary tale and a how-to as well, *Love and Struggle* is a book as candid, as uncompromising, and as humane as its author.

Praise:

"Gilbert adds heart and bone to the stuff of history." —Mumia Abu-Jamal

"Required reading for anyone interested in the history of radical movements in this country. An honest, vivid portrait of a life spent passionately fighting for justice. In telling his story, Gilbert also reveals the history of left struggles in the 1960s and 70s, and imparts important lessons for today's activists." —Jordan Flaherty, author of *Floodlines: Community and Resistance from Katrina to the Jena Six*

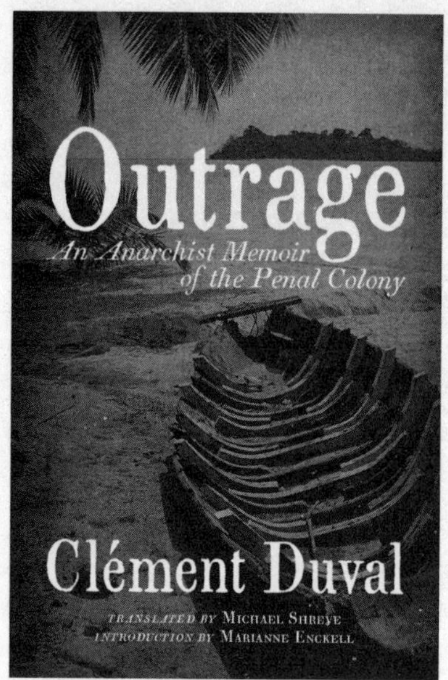

ALSO AVAILABLE FROM PM PRESS

Outrage: An Anarchist Memoir of the Penal Colony
by Clément Duval
ISBN: 978-1-60486-500-4
$20.00

"Theft exists only through the exploitation of man by man…when Society refuses you the right to exist, you must take it…the policeman arrested me in the name of the Law, I struck him in the name of Liberty."

In 1887, Clément Duval joined the tens of thousands of convicts sent to the "dry guillotine" of the French penal colonies. Few survived and fewer were able to tell the stories of their life in that hell. Duval spent fourteen years doing hard labor—espousing the values of anarchism and demonstrating the ideals by being a living example the entire time—before making his daring escape and arriving in New York City, welcomed by the Italian and French anarchists there.

This is much more than an historical document about the anarchist movement and the penal colony. It is a remarkable story of survival by one man's self-determination, energy, courage, loyalty, and hope. It was thanks to being true and faithful to his ideals that Duval survived life in this hell. Unlike the well-known prisoner Papillon, who arrived and dramatically escaped soon after Duval, he encouraged his fellow prisoners to practice mutual aid, through their deeds and not just their words. It is a call to action for mindful, conscious people to fight for their rights to the very end, to never give up or give in.

More than just a story of a life or a testament of ideals, here is a monument to the human spirit and a war cry for freedom and justice.

About Clément Duval:

Clément Duval (1850–1935) was an infamous French illegalist, propagandist, and anarchist who was found guilty in 1886 of theft and attempted murder of a police officer. Originally sentenced to death, his sentence was commuted to deportation and hard labor in the French Guiana prison camps. After fourteen years and twenty escape attempts, Duval and fellow inmates set out on a rickety boat. He eventually reached New York City in 1901 and was welcomed by French and Italian anarchists. In 1929 Italian anarchist Luigi Galleani translated and published his full memoirs as *Memorie autobiografiche.*

ALSO AVAILABLE FROM PM PRESS

The Real Cost Of Prisons Comix
Edited by Lois Ahrens
ISBN: 978-1-60486-034-4
$14.95

Winner of the 2008 PASS Award (Prevention for a Safer Society) from the National Council on Crime and Delinquency

One out of every hundred adults in the U.S. is in prison. This book provides a crash course in what drives mass incarceration, the human and community costs, and how to stop the numbers from going even higher. This volume collects the three comic books published by the Real Cost of Prisons Project. The stories and statistical information in each comic book is thoroughly researched and documented.

Prison Town: Paying the Price tells the story of how the financing and site locations of prisons affects the people of rural communities in which prison are built. It also tells the story of how mass incarceration affects people of urban communities where the majority of incarcerated people come from.

Prisoners of the War on Drugs includes the history of the war on drugs, mandatory minimums, how racism creates harsher sentences for people of color, stories on how the war on drugs works against women, three strikes laws, obstacles to coming home after incarceration, and how mass incarceration destabilizes neighborhoods.

Prisoners of a Hard Life: Women and Their Children includes stories about women trapped by mandatory sentencing and the "costs" of incarceration for women and their families. Also included are alternatives to the present system, a glossary, and footnotes.

Praise:

"I cannot think of a better way to arouse the public to the cruelties of the prison system than to make this book widely available." —Howard Zinn

STAUGHTON LYND

ACCOMPANYING

PATHWAYS TO SOCIAL CHANGE

ALSO AVAILABLE FROM PM PRESS

Accompanying: Pathways to Social Change
by Staughton Lynd
ISBN: 978-1-60486-666-7
$14.95

In *Accompanying*, Staughton Lynd distinguishes two strategies of social change. The first, characteristic of the 1960s Movement in the United States, is "organizing." The second, articulated by Archbishop Oscar Romero of El Salvador, is "accompaniment." The critical difference is that in accompanying one another the promoter of social change and his or her oppressed colleague view themselves as two experts, each bringing indispensable experience to a shared project. Together, as equals, they seek to create what the Zapatistas call "another world."

Staughton Lynd applies the distinction between organizing and accompaniment to five social movements in which he has taken part: the labor and civil rights movements, the antiwar movement, prisoner insurgencies, and the movement sparked by Occupy Wall Street. His wife Alice Lynd, a partner in these efforts, contributes her experience as a draft counselor and advocate for prisoners in maximum-security confinement.

Praise:

"Since our dreams for a more just world came crashing down around us in the late 1980s and early 1990s, those of us involved in social activism have spent much of the time since trying to assess what went wrong and what we might learn from our mistakes. In this highly readable book, Lynd explores the difference between organizing and accompanying. This book is a must read for anyone who believes a better world is possible." —Margaret Randall

"Everything that Staughton Lynd writes is original and provocative. This little book is no exception. Among his greatest contributions on display here is the transformation of the 'organizer' and 'organized' into a collaboration of different people with different skills, each making a decisive contribution." —Paul Buhle, author of *Robin Hood: People's Outlaw and Forest Hero*

ALSO AVAILABLE FROM PM PRESS

A History of Pan-African Revolt
by C.L.R. James
ISBN: 978-1-60486-095-5
$16.95

Originally published in England in 1938 (the same year as his magnum opus *The Black Jacobins*) and expanded in 1969, this work remains the classic account of global Black Resistance. Robin D.G. Kelley's substantial introduction contextualizes the work in the history and ferment of the times, and explores its ongoing relevance today.

"*A History of Pan-African Revolt* is one of those rare books that continues to strike a chord of urgency, even half a century after it was first published. Time and time again, its lessons have proven to be valuable and relevant for understanding liberation movements in Africa and the diaspora. Each generation who has had the opportunity to read this small book finds new insights, new lessons, new visions for their own age.... No piece of literature can substitute for a crystal ball, and only religious fundamentalists believe that a book can provide comprehensive answers to all questions. But if nothing else, *A History of Pan-African Revolt* leaves us with two incontrovertible facts. First, as long as Black people are denied freedom, humanity and a decent standard of living, they will continue to revolt. Second, unless these revolts involve the ordinary masses and take place on their own terms, they have no hope of succeeding."
—From the Introduction by Robin D.G. Kelley

Praise:

"Kudos for reissuing C.L.R. James's pioneering work on Black resistance. Many brilliant embryonic ideas articulated in *A History Of Pan-African Revolt* twenty years later became the way to study Black social movements. Robin Kelley's introduction superbly situates James and his thought in the world of Pan-African and Marxist intellectuals."
—Sundiata Cha-Jua, Penn State University

"A mine of ideas advancing far ahead of its time."
—Walter Rodney

ALSO AVAILABLE FROM PM PRESS & COMMON NOTIONS

Revolution at Point Zero: Housework, Reproduction, and Feminist Struggle
by Silvia Federici
ISBN: 978-1-60486-333-8
$15.95

Written between 1974 and the present, *Revolution at Point Zero* collects forty years of research and theorizing on the nature of housework, social reproduction, and women's struggles on this terrain—to escape it, to better its conditions, to reconstruct it in ways that provide an alternative to capitalist relations.

Indeed, as Federici reveals, behind the capitalist organization of work and the contradictions inherent in "alienated labor" is an explosive ground zero for revolutionary practice upon which are decided the daily realities of our collective reproduction.

Beginning with Federici's organizational work in the Wages for Housework movement, the essays collected here unravel the power and politics of wide but related issues including the international restructuring of reproductive work and its effects on the sexual division of labor, the globalization of care work and sex work, the crisis of elder care, the development of affective labor, and the politics of the commons.

Praise:

"Finally we have a volume that collects the many essays that over a period of four decades Silvia Federici has written on the question of social reproduction and women's struggles on this terrain. While providing a powerful history of the changes in the organization of reproductive labor, Revolution at Point Zero documents the development of Federici's thought on some of the most important questions of our time: globalization, gender relations, the construction of new commons." —Mariarosa Dalla Costa, coauthor of *The Power of Women and the Subversion of the Community* and *Our Mother Ocean*